Thomas Jondrie Vivian

The Fall of Santiago

Thomas Jondrie Vivian

The Fall of Santiago

ISBN/EAN: 9783744653152

Printed in Europe, USA, Canada, Australia, Japan

Cover: Foto ©ninafisch / pixelio.de

More available books at **www.hansebooks.com**

THE
FALL OF SANTIAGO

BY
THOMAS J. VIVIAN
Author of "With Dewey at Manila."

R. F. FENNO & COMPANY : 9 AND 11 E.
SIXTEENTH STREET : : NEW YORK
1898

Copyright, 1898
BY
R. F. FENNO & COMPANY

The Fall of Santiago

CONTENTS.

CHAPTER I.
How Schley Chased Cervera's Fleet........ 5

CHAPTER II.
How Hobson Sank the Merrimac.................... 25

CHAPTER III.
How the Marines Fought at Guantanamo............ 51

CHAPTER IV.
How Shafter Landed His Army at Daiquiri.......... 72

CHAPTER V.
How the Rough Riders Fought at La Guasima........ 95

CHAPTER VI.
How the Army Marched to the Front................ 112

CHAPTER VII.
How El Caney Was Carried......................... 133

CHAPTER VIII.
How San Juan Was Stormed and Taken.............. 155

CHAPTER IX.
How Schley Destroyed Cervera's Fleet............... 190

CHAPTER X.
How Toral Surrendered More than was Asked for.... 227

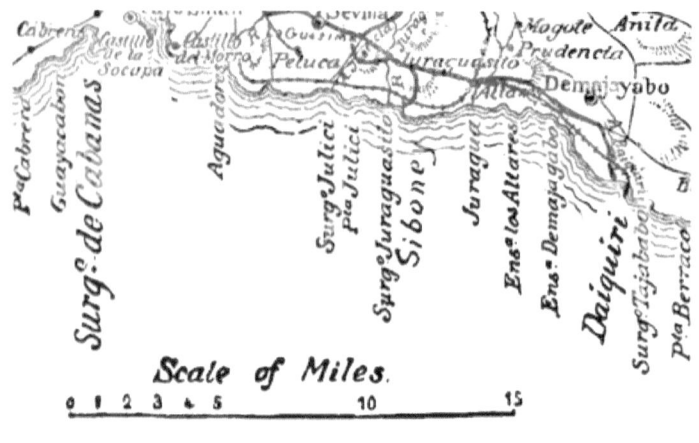

Military operations around Santiago.
indicate their importance as ways of travel, but, for the purpose of identification.

THE FALL OF SANTIAGO.

CHAPTER I.

HOW SCHLEY CHASED CERVERA'S FLEET.

At the time that the great sea hunt for Admiral Cervera's elusive fleet began, the condition of things specifically hinging on it was just this:

There were three positive and five possible parties in the hunt. The positive parties were Schley's Flying Squadron, then a resting one at Hampton Roads; Sampson's Blockading Fleet, off Havana; and Admiral Cervera's Cape Verde Squadron, so called because at the outbreak of hostilities the Spanish ships constituting that squadron were at the Cape Verde Islands. The possibilities were Admiral Camara's fleet at Cadiz and Admiral Villamil's squadron, concerning whose exact location there existed much doubt. Ever since the 25th of April, the date of the declaration of war between the United States and Spain, it was a self-evident strategical proposition that no definite campaign in the West

Indies could be laid out and carried through until an accounting had been made with the Spanish fleet or fleets.

In general: The blockade of Havana was established; the presidential policy was esteemed from the outside to be one of pacific waiting; Admiral Dewey had destroyed the Spanish fleet at Manila; and Spain was threatening to send a heavy sea force against him in the hope of regaining her power in the Orient. Troops were gathering from every part of the United States toward the fields of Chickamauga and the blazing sand spits and coral keys of Florida; the different States had been called on to send their quota of volunteers to the front; and the government agents were busy all over the world buying war ships and craft convertible into cruisers.

Such was the naval and military status when late on the night of May 12 Commodore Schley walked into his cabin on the Brooklyn with an unopened dispatch in his hands, which dispatch had just been brought out from Fortress Monroe. An hour after, it being then exactly one A.M., May 13, a string of colored lights was displayed from the flagship, "Be ready to put to sea at daybreak." Evidently there were many wakeful eyes on the fleet, and no sooner had the commodore's signal gone up than a whole colony of drug stores seemed to spring into being as the colored lights were run up all around with the answer "Signal understood. We will be ready."

There was no more sleep that night on board the fleet, and although they did not sail at daybreak, the executive officers made the effort of their lives to do so. The laggards in this case were the converted cruiser St. Paul and the cruiser New Orleans which were coaling at Newport News. The squadron waited, to the visible heat and audible impatience of the commodore, until half-past three in the afternoon, and then, accompanied by a big collier, the Brooklyn, Massachusetts, Texas, Minneapolis and Scorpion sailed, leaving instructions for the St. Paul and New Orleans to follow as quickly as they could.

Save for the delay there was jollity all over the fleet, for though the men were not sure what they were going to do, they were certain that they were going to do something, and that they had two hundred guns of the most modern type, eighteen hundred officers and men, and seven good vessels to do it with.

Next day, that is May 14, the squadron was off Charleston and there it was found that the sealed orders under which sail was made from Hampton Roads, read only to put to sea at once and proceed to Charleston, there to receive further orders. It may be said here, and with much appropriateness, that rarely for an instant was there any evidence of indecision on the part of those in control of the Santiago campaign and that with few exceptions the plans that were made were clear, were expressed to those who had to discharge them with equal clearness, and carried out as undeviatingly as the changing circumstances of war would permit by those in command of the operations on land and sea. At Charleston the new orders were to proceed to Havana with all expedition there to join forces with Admiral Sampson, under whose command two fast fleets would be made up for the Cervera hunt.

But while the plans of the hunters were known with some kind of definiteness those of the quarry were decidedly nebulous. The Dons were rich in what may be called the feint and ambuscade of news. The Cape Verde Fleet had sailed. It had not sailed. It was at the Canaries. It was at Cadiz. These were some of the sample reports. Of course, at Washington data of a somewhat more definite character had been gathered by trusted agents, but so wily and uncertain, so full of dodges, turns, back-tracking and unexpected dashes was Cervera at the last that not the combined intelligence of the Secr.

Admiral Cevera.

Service branches of the War and Navy Departments and the untiring and omnipresent newspaper men could always tell where Spain's greatest of naval dodgers really was.

The facts that were patent were these. When the war broke out Cervera, as has been said, was at St. Vincent in the Cape de Verde Islands. Now these islands belong to Portugal and it was intimated to Portugal by our State Department that the presence of Cervera's fleet, coupled with the ostentatious announcement that Spain intended to gather at St. Vincent one of those formidable armadas which have ever been her pet embodiment of naval power, would seem to indicate that the nation with which we were at war was using the territory of a nation with which we were at peace as a base of offensive operations and we would like to know just what Portugal's position in the matter was. In answer to this demand Portugal's prime minister cabled to the State Department at Washington, April 26, that the Spanish flotilla would be given forty-eight hours in which to leave St. Vincent.

When the forty-eight hours were up, however, the Spanish flotilla was still at St. Vincent. Then, on April 28, Portugal, in response to another quiet but still more emphatic interrogatory from Washington as to her position, did declare her neutrality, and Cervera, having in this friendly leisure mobilized his fleet and thoroughly provisioned and coaled it, soon after steamed away with his black-painted warships. But with the certainty of Cervera's departure ended the certainty of his whereabouts, and it was from the latter date that the Cervera hunt may be said to properly begin.

Would he sail back to Cadiz to join forces with Camara? Would he sail to the Canaries, there to wait until reinforced by Admiral Villamil with his undefined fleet? Was he planning to intercept the battleship Oregon on her great trip around Cape Horn and crush her by force of numbers? Would he make a dash for the North Atlantic ports; reduce the summer cottages of Newport to ruins; loot the Boston banks of their millions; or, dashing down Long Island Sound, lay Brooklyn waste and raze New York's sky scrapers to the ground? Was Newport News, with its yards and government supplies to be captured? Was Charleston in danger or Key West to be bombarded? Did the Spanish admiral contemplate a flight across the Atlantic to Porto Rico with a view of using that port as a strong base for menace and attack? Would he push on through the Carribean Sea and get into the shelter of Cienfuegos, with its railroad to

Havana, and so bring new heart and supplies to Governor-General Blanco; or would he make one wild cut at the blockading squadron and try to get into Havana itself? All of these propositions had to be considered and though some were wild, none could be dismissed as impossible.

It may be asked why Cervera's fleet was considered such an important factor; why the programme of the United States depended so much on the disposal of the Cape Verde flotilla and why the plan was not adopted to quietly wait until Cervera's fleet materialized and then meet and smash it. The answer is a plain one. When Cervera left St. Vincent his fleet consisted of four first-class cruisers—the Vizcaya, the Almirante Oquendo, the Cristobal Colon and the Infanta Maria Teresa; and three torpedo boat destroyers, the Furor, the Terror, and the Pluton. Not such a formidable fleet, one might imagine, considering the fact that Schley's flying squadron included the Massachusetts, Texas, Brooklyn, New Orleans, and Minneapolis; that Sampson from his blockaders could make up a fighting fleet consisting of the Iowa, Indiana, New York, Amphitrite, Terror, Detroit, Montgomery, and Marblehead; and that if he had luck, Captain Clark could join these with the Oregon, Marietta and Nictheroy. The potent fact about Cervera's fleet, however, was its homogeneity. It was all alike. In a collection of fighting vessels, as in a collection of fighting men, its unit of capability is its weak spot. When moving into action or retiring from one, the fastest cruiser can only sail at the speed of the slowest—that is, if there is to be any concert of attack or retreat. The four cruisers of Cervera were not only all alike in speed, they were all alike in strength, in the disposition, art of training and power of their batteries. The tonnage of the Cristobal Colon was 6,840 while that of the other three cruisers was exactly 6,890 for each vessel. The Colon's batteries could throw in one ton of metal at each volley, while the volley of the other three was one and a quarter tons each. The speed of each ship was twenty knots.

It follows, then, that the four cruisers might practically be considered as one enormous fighting machine, with equal power to strike, speed to run, strength to resist and which, if properly handled, would really be one of the most formidable things afloat. It must not be inferred from all this that there would be any hesitation on the part of our fleet commanders to engage Cervera as soon as found, but it must be understood that Cervera afloat and unsmashed was a menace of formidable proportions.

Com. Winfield Scott Schley.

The Fall of Santiago.

Instructions having been received to proceed to Key West, to Key West Schley's squadron sailed. That scorched end of the United States was reached on May 18 and next day the commodore was joined by Admiral Sampson and his fleet. Sampson had been off on an errand of his own and though it had been moderately successful in one way, it had been a failure in another and he was not in the most cheerful of moods when Schley went to visit him. His double purpose when he drew away from the blockading fleet outside Havana had been to chase down Cervera, and failing that, to put Porto Rico into such an undefendable condition that the Spanish admiral might not be able to use it as a harbor of refuge. He did not engage the Spaniard and so on May 9 reported to Washington an inability to find any trace of Spain's master in the art of hiding, and announced his intention to bombard Porto Rico. That intention he carried into partial effect on the 12th of May, but of what was done on that date and in that action it would be too wide a parenthesis to speak here.

After thoroughly canvassing the situation and as a result of the combined capital of information possessed by the admiral and commodore and furnished them from Washington, it was decided that instead of combining the fleets for a further sea hunt the vessels under command of Sampson and Schley should be divided and two lines of pursuit followed. Sampson held that he had given Porto Rico such a shaking up that it was in no condition to afford anything except the shakiest kind of support to Cervera; that the Spanish admiral would not think of remaining there when once he discovered its condition; and that so much, therefore, in the twistings and doublings of the pursued fleet might be eliminated.

There remained then, the dash on the Atlantic ports, the endeavor to force the blockade of Havana, the push ahead for a port on the southern coast of Cuba or the double and return flight to Cadiz. As to the ports on the southern coast of Cuba there were only two which were thought necessary of consideration—those of Cienfuegos and Santiago. Of these the balance of opinion was that everything was in favor of Cervera's selection lighting upon Cienfuegos. It lies right across from Havana on the southern coast, has an excellent harbor, and, as has been intimated, is within easy railroad connection with the Cuban capital. Then, too, it was one of the places on which a blockade had been set, so that if the Spanish Admiral contemplated any scheme of relief Cienfuegos was the best place for its application. The fortifications of Cien-

The Fall of Santiago.

fuegos were not as formidable, it is true, as they had been prior to May 14, when Commander McCalla, with the cruisers Marblehead and Nashville and the converted cruiser Windom, sent one of the big guns there sprawling, rent the forts at the harbor's entrance with four and six-inch shells, and left things generally demoralized after a three hours' administration of iron and steel correctives. McCalla's object had been to cut the cable between Cienfuegos and Manzanillo and the ripping bombardment, which lasted from six to nine A.M. was inflicted because the Spanish forts had fired on the American boats while they were engaged in this enterprise. Still, Cienfuegos ranked as a fortified and very enticing haven for Cervera, and it was decided that leaving Commodore Watson to continue the blockade of Havana with his "mosquito fleet," Schley should sail around the western end of Cuba to that port, while Sampson was to sail eastward down to the Windward Passage, so as to intercept Cervera should he try to make for Havana and at the same time to trap him should he have visited Porto Rico and found it untenable.

Commodore Schley sailed from Key West on May 19, taking with him the Brooklyn, Texas, Massachusetts, and Scorpion. These reached

Cienfuegos Sunday, May 22, and were there joined by the Iowa, the cruiser Marblehead, the torpedo boat Dupont, the gunboats Castine and Eagle, and the collier Merrimac, the latter craft, which was destined to become historical, having arrived at eight o'clock on the morning of May 23 under the convoy of the Castine. When Cienfuegos was reached it was seen that much work of reparation had been done on the fortifications at the harbor mouth, so much indeed that even after the peppering which McCalla had administered it would have been no easy task to force a way past the batteries at Punta Colorado on the one hand, and the much more important fortification at the castle of Xagua on the other. Many contradictory reports were brought the commodore by Cuban scouts as to the presence of Cervera in Cienfuegos, the general trend of these reports, however, being that the Spanish admiral had arrived and was safely ensconced behind these fortifications. Schley was much inclined to the opinion that he had run down the Spanish admiral and had indeed prepared a report to that effect when the little gunboat Hawk, a converted yacht, brought such definite news of Cervera being really at Santiago, that he had to accept it as authoritative. He would have started for Santiago there and then, but the

Castle of El Morro, the eastern guardian of the sea gateway to Santiago.

The Fall of Santiago.

question of coaling—the pivotal question in naval proceedings nowadays—delayed him until Tuesday.

With Schley at Cienfuegos preparing to run down to Santiago to establish the accuracy of the Hawk's report; with Sampson cruising along the northern coast of Cuba and watching the Windward Passage, with the Yale and St. Louis, auxiliary cruisers, scouting and watching for Cervera at the Mona and Virgin Passages, and with half a dozen other scouts steaming here and there over the Atlantic and West Indian seas, it will be appropriate here to show how Cervera eluded his pursuers. And as it happened, it was by one of the strange fortunes of war that the exact story came to light through the capture of the flagship's log-book, as the Cristobal Colon lay a battered and stranded hulk off Santiago's rocky shore.

It will be remembered that Portugal informed our government that Cervera had been instructed to vacate his anchorage on April 26 with a forty-eight hours time of grace, he having arrived there on the 14th. As a matter of fact, Cervera left St. Vincent, April 30, the Colon towing the Furor, the Oquendo the Pluton, and the Teresa the Terror. When Cervera left he steamed westward. The next report was from Spain, that

Cervera had returned home and that on May 11 he was safe at Cadiz, waiting to be reinforced by Admiral Camara's ships. Here again the truth is that on that very day he was within twenty-four hour's easy steam of Port de France, Martinique. Waiting at Port de France only for dispatches, he pushed on southwestward, and on Saturday, May 14, reached Willemstad, the port of the Dutch island of Curacao. He entered the harbor with the Teresa and Vizcaya, leaving the Oquendo and Colon, with the three torpedo boat destroyers on the outside. The selection of Willemstad as a port of call, while at first blush it may seem to have been an out-of-the-way locality, was really an excellent one. The French cable for Caracas, Venezuela, touches at Curacao, so that he was able to communicate with home over a friendly line and at the same time be posted as to the condition of things in Cuba.

It doubtless had been Cervera's original plan to steam swiftly over the four hundred and seventy-five miles lying between Curacao and Porto Rico, and establish there a base of supplies and attack, but at the Dutch settlement he learned of Sampson's attentions to Porto Rico, and so having given out the intimation that he intended under the new condition of things, to

The Fall of Santiago.

keep in the friendly shelter of the South American shores, sent the Terror on a scouting trip to Porto Rico, steamed away westward, then retraced his way, put on all steam and crowded for Santiago, which he reached on the morning of May 19.

The prosaic but essential work of coaling having been completed, Schley shipped anchor off Cienfuegos and steamed eastward. He was off Santiago on May 28, but neither from his guns nor from the shore batteries was a single shot fired to emphasize the fact of his arrival.

It will not be going ahead of the proper sequence of fact and description to say here that the presence of Cervera's fleet in the harbor of Santiago, as something that could be sworn to from evidence of sight was an extremely difficult matter of demonstration. Like all of the harbors along the Cuban coast, that of Santiago is bottle-shaped, with the neck as the entrance. But in the case of Santiago there is not only a neck, but a long and curved one. Moreover the shore sides of the neck entrance are so high and precipitous that from the sea it is impossible to look into the harbor beyond that part which lies close to the inner end of the neck. How to satisfy himself that Cervera was at Santiago without sailing into the harbor presented itself, therefore, as the problem which Schley would have to solve. To risk a sharp dash into the harbor with all its certain dangers and its uncertainties, its tortuous channel, mines and commanding fortifications, with the chance of not finding the quarry in the presumptive hiding-place, was something about which even Schley hestitated. There remained then strategy, and that strategy the commodore employed.

Schley knew as well as though he had been told by the Governor of Santiago that his movements were being closely watched from the shore, that indeed no move was made without being known and its significance noted. As soon therefore as the squadron had steamed into the blue water that lay in the bight of land forming what might be called the Bay of Santiago, it steamed slowly around, past the harbor mouth, close enough to distinguish the guns in the forts. Again no gun was fired. Upon reaching the extreme eastern limit of the bight the squadron was formed in line and steamed away westward as though it had been making merely a reconnaissance. The presumption was that if Cervera were in the long-necked and land-locked harbor of Santiago he would, if the feint were successful, move down toward the mouth to help resist the invader, and so come into the line of vision.

High altar in the Cathedral at Santiago where a Te Deum was sung on the arrival of Cervera's fleet.

The Fall of Santiago. 21

Steaming away westward with as near an air of disgust and disappointment as it was possible for a squadron to assume, Schley signaled to stop when at a sufficient distance, it being then one o'clock on Saturday afternoon, and the vessels hid themselves, so to speak, behind a point of land that shut out all observation from the Santiago lookouts.

When Sunday morning broke, and Sunday seems to have been selected as the day of deeds in this war, all steam was made and the squadron went churning its way back to Santiago. Putting the keenest-eyed men aloft and arming himself with the biggest pair of binoculars that the ship possessed, the commodore went on the bridge and headed the flagship full speed for the harbor entrance. Through his glasses he made out the earthworks and the Spaniards behind them, but no glimpse of vessels could he get. When five miles from the shore the lookouts reported the masts of three ships peeping over the entrance cliffs. This was promising, but the commodore wanted to see for himself.

Next Flag-Lieutenant Sears and Ensign McCalley, who were perched in the forward fighting top, declared they could see the vessels, and that one of them was the Cristobal Colon. Still Schley kept the vessel moving, and a few minutes later word was shouted down from aloft that two torpedo boats and a vessel of the Vizcaya class could be seen. Still the Brooklyn was kept on its course, until for an instant it lay right in a direct line of sight into the harbor. In that happy moment the commodore saw that his ruse had been successful, for there clustering about the inside of the entrance was Cervera's fleet.

As the Brooklyn was turned quickly out, Schley took down his glasses and with a wink of most portentous satisfaction said:

"I told you I would find them. I have caught them and they will never get home."

Gratified as the commodore was, and as all his men were, at the finding of Cervera's fleet, this pacific end of the chase by no means gratified the sailors and the fighting men of the deck. The batteries had been cleared, the men stripped for action, and though the temperature was a hundred degrees in the shade, the sailors were hotter still to fight. But Schley believed that it was no time for a fight. For three days a howling storm with furious gusts of rain-laden wind had been sweeping this southeastern shore, the great ships were heaving and bumping in the cross running waves, and as an effective bombardment is difficult enough under the best conditions, it was Schley's opinion that he might rest content with the discovery of Cervera as the final act of this edition of the play, without risking an anti-climax by firing shells around Santiago's forts.

Having found him, however, the commodore was very determined not to let Cervera escape, and Sunday evening, May 29, found our squadron in battle line outside Santiago, the Brooklyn on the east of the line, then the Massachusetts, the Iowa, the New Orleans (Amazonas) and the Texas, while the Marblehead and Vixen scouted near the shore and the Harvard was racing over to Kingston to cable the news to Washington.

Cervera and his twenty-million-dollars' worth of cruisers had been found.

Madrid, it was learned afterward, characterized Cervera's slip into Santiago as a remarkable piece of strategy and a tactician's victory. Santiago welcomed Cervera as the city's savior. The whole community turned out to welcome the admiral; there was band-playing, song-singing, speech-making, fireworks and a Te Deum of thankfulness at the cathedral with the Archbishop Monsignor Saenz y Utero y Crespo officiating in his most gorgeous raiment. At Washington the receipt of the news was regarded as having cleared up the entire situation, and as dispelling the clouds of uncertainty which had been over the War and Navy Department for weeks. It meant a radical change in the plan of campaign, but that change was from the general to the particular. It crystallized the operations into the specific act of capturing or destroying Cervera's fleet and possibly the investment and capture of Santiago.

With the sun setting of Sunday, May 29, the wind went down also, and there could be heard the great diapason of the Texas men singing the hymn "Pull for the Shore," and as he heard it Schley again winked that portentous wink of his and said: "We'll be pulling there, sure enough, in a few days."

CHAPTER II.

HOW HOBSON SANK THE MERRIMAC.

WASHINGTON's reply to Schley's notification of having found Cervera was:

"Under no circumstances permit ships to escape. Destroy or capture them."

And as the circling events proved, the commodore carried out those instructions to the letter.

Soon after this order reached Schley, he was joined, Wednesday morning, June 1, by Sampson with the New York, Oregon and Mayflower, and later by the torpedo boat Porter, the Dolphin and the Adria with supplies and appliances for grappling and cutting marine cables. Schley went on board the New York to report, and it was thought that the conference would result in some decided action. Schley related what has been told here, and in addition told of the capture of Cervera's coal ship, the Restormel, by Captain Sigsbee of the St. Paul, under the very guns of Santiago's El Morro on the 25th of May; of the bombardment of Santiago on May

31, in which the batteries of Punta Gorda, El Morro and Zacopa were furiously shelled, and so the commodore believed, a Spanish cruiser disabled. He thought at the time that it was the Cristobal Colon, but it was learned afterward that it was the old timer Reina Mercedes which had been lying at Santiago. It was learned, too, that a shell from the Massachusetts had struck this cruiser, which had been drawn up behind the harbor entrance as a sort of floating battery, and, exploding, had partially sunk the ancient craft. Schley was not very enthusiastic over the result of this bombardment, and frankly stated that when he withdrew at six o'clock in the evening the Zacopa and Punta Gorda batteries were still firing. He therefore counseled that if it were decided to force an entrance into Santiago and engage Cervera a necessary preliminary would be to increase the blockading fleet with four monitors and the Helena, the Wilmington, the Cincinnati, the Montgomery, the Detroit and the dynamite boat the Vesuvius—especially the latter—as with her dynamite bombs she might explode the mines along the entrance way and so clear a passage into the harbor after silencing the forts.

Sampson held, however, and that without in the faintest discrediting the report of the com-

The Fall of Santiago. 27

modore, that the absolute identification of Cervera's fleet was first necessary, and the identification being complete, the bottling up of that fleet might be tried in a somewhat original and spectacular fashion. The following out of these two ideas brought into the fierce light of fame two young men, Lieutenant Victor Blue, of the gunboat Suwanee, and Naval Constructor, Richmond Pierson Hobson.

In the matter of occurrence, as well as in the relatively momentous results, the enterprise of Hobson comes easily first. But lest that of Blue should be lost sight of in the brighter light of that which enhaloes Hobson, the expedition of the lieutenant shall be dealt with first.

To catch a glimpse of the masts of warships through the sinuous entrance to Santiago harbor, and to look down on those warships from the heights surrounding Santiago at such a distance as would make their identification absolute, were rightly esteemed by Sampson as two entirely different propositions; the one being burdened with the element of doubt, the other being endowed with the benefit of certainty. Admiral Sampson therefore determined to send a man on a trip of inspection, and the man he selected for this enterprise was Lieutenant Blue, who had already run the gauntlet of five Spanish gunboats in the bay of Buena Vista, and had carried the American flag to the spot of his meeting with General Gomez.

On Saturday, June 11, Blue was landed in a little cove well to the east of the entrance and pushing his way through a country swarming with Spanish soldiery, and through the sweltering, tangled jungle, only halted when he peered through the cacti and palms which crested a hill overlooking the old city and the long blue bay. In the bay he saw Cervera's fleet, four armored cruisers, two torpedo boat destroyers, and the wrecked Reina Mercedes, which with a gunboat had constituted Santiago's naval defense before the arrival of Cervera. Then backward through the sweltering jungle, dodging the Spanish outposts and wriggling his way through a network of tangling vines and tearing thorns, until on Monday, ragged but triumphant, he stood on the quarter-deck of the flagship New York and made his report to Admiral Sampson.

Seventy-two miles of travel through an enemy's country and a pathless tropical thicket, is a deed which in times of ordinary enterprise would stand out as a matter for a volume, but when writing of these stirring times when every day saw something done that marked the upspringing of a new hero, Lieutenant Blue's gallant work must be dismissed with a paragraph. It is the misfortune of comparison which diminishes the fact.

So many, many things have been written and said and sung about Hobson, and how he put the stopper into the Santiago bottle that all there remains to do is to tell a clear running story of the actual facts, even at the risk of brushing aside one or two illusions, but, of course, without minifying the heroism of accomplishment.

When sailing eastward along the northern coast of Cuba the contingencies of Cervera's capture were more than once discussed on board Sampson's flagship—so Sampson reported to Washington—and it was during one of these discussions that the admiral said:

"I think it quite possible we shall find that Cervera has made a running for it to Santiago harbor. If so, and if Schley has him shut up there I am in favor of closing the door of his prison house rather than of attempting to batter down the door-post."

When asked what this plan might be the admiral replied that it was not quite formulated, but that it embraced the sinking of an obstruction in the mouth of the harbor, "And by the by," he added, "young Hobson, of the Construction Bureau, is just the man I want to consult with. I noticed him at San Juan when he stood at our range-finder timing the shells."

Hobson was sent for and to him was put the proposition of "making the harbor entrance secure against the possibilities of egress by the Spanish ships by obstructing the narrow part of the entrance" to quote Sampson's words. Hobson at once took the liveliest interest in the plan and asked for a day or two in which to consider the problem and the best means of working it out. At the end of the given time Hobson reported to the admiral. His plan briefly was not to wait for stone-laden barges, which had been suggested as the best form of impediment, but to take one of the fleet colliers and sink her athwart the selected place in the channel. Hobson showed that the drawbacks to the barge scheme were the time it would take to get them from a United States port, and the fact that they would have to be towed into position, while in the case of the collier there would be no delay and she would have the added advantage of being a self-propelling engine. Hobson wound up by entering a plea that to him might be intrusted the active carrying out of the plan.

"You know all that this means, Hobson?" asked the admiral.

"I do, sir," replied Hobson; and the admiral consented.

No one who knew Hobson could very well see

how the admiral could have refused. Upright as one of his own Alabama pines; twenty-eight years old; ruggedly simple in his manners; with dogged determination expressed in every feature, from the deep set eyes, along the pronounced bridge of the nose down to the square-set jaw; the sweetheart of his mother; not afraid to show that he carried a Bible in his kit; a student, equally ready to pray or to fight, and with a long record of having done both, "Rich" Hobson was just the sort of man that any other man would have selected for the short and fiery cruise of the Merrimac.

Sampson, it will be remembered, joined Schley off Santiago on Wednesday morning, June 1, and immediately on receiving Schley's report sent in his launch to reconnoiter ashore. The report brought back confirmed Schley's estimates of the difficulties of running the forts and crystalized his resolution to attempt the bottling-up process and to attempt it at once.

The collier Merrimac was selected for the office of barrier. A Norwegian steam freighter, called the Solveid; three hundred and forty-four feet long, and with a tonnage of five thousand three hundred and sixty-two tons; burned out while loading grain at Newport News, April 27, 1897; repaired at the Erie Basin, Brooklyn, for the

Lone Star Line, and standing to that company at one hundred and ninety-two thousand dollars; sold to the government for three hundred and forty-two thousand dollars; no beauty and generally cantankerous in her behavior—not a soul grieved when her selection for sacrifice was announced.

As soon as the selection was made, active work was begun to fix her up for the slaughter. All her stores were taken out and all of her coal except two thousand tons. In the engine room, not to be technical, the covers to the valves of the big fire pump were so arranged that a single blow of a sledge would let in the sea; all watertight doors were opened, and where possible, the bulkheads were broken down so as to give free play to the water as soon as it was admitted into the ship. The salient part of the plan was to scuttle her by outside explosion and as a means to this end, ten pitch covered 8-inch copper cases, each filled with eighty pounds of ordinary brown, prismatic powder and each fitted with an igniting charge, primer and connecting wire for electrically exploding the charge, were lowered over the port rail until they rested against the side of the vessel just below the water line; the charges being so arranged that in each case they would bear their explosive force against the space between the bulkheads.

When the bombs had been lowered into position, the wires for exploding the charges were run along the deck and connected with a main wire leading to a dry battery and contact key on the bridge. Lastly, in the way of preparation for sinking her all her ports were lashed open and the four cargo ports (the openings in the sides of the ship through which a cargo is taken on while the vessel is lying at her dock) were opened, two forward and two aft, there being about three feet of freeboard from the water to the lower edge of the cargo ports—that is, that as the vessel lay drawing sixteen feet of water these openings were nineteen feet above her keel.

All these preparations meant that, were they successfully and simultaneously carried out, at the touch of the key and the blow of the sledge hammer, six great gaping holes would be torn in the ship's sides, the great sea valves would be opened, and as the vessel shuddered and rocked under the explosion the sea would rush into her and, thus inundated from stem to stern by twleve rushing cataracts of water, the Merrimac would go down like a rock dropped from a cliff into the sea. Lastly, as the plan for bringing her to a sudden halt at the desired locality, both of the ship's anchors were lashed over the rail at the starboard quarter in such a way that the chop of an ax would cut the lashings and drop them in an instant. Then, not that there was very much hope that they would be used, but as a Christian precaution, a lifeboat and a catamaran life raft were slung over the side by steel lines and a ship's launch was to be detailed to follow in the wake and pick up the survivors of this Enterprise Perilous.

All day long two hundred men were busy as bees stripping the Merrimac and preparing her for her last trip. From first to last, and that without any planning on the part of the participators, the incident of the Merrimac was most spectacular. As the men pulled and tore and dragged at their work of discharging the collier Merrimac and charging her as a death machine, they sang sometimes cheerily, sometimes dolefully; and as they sang and worked, one of those black rattling thunderstorms which punctuate Cuba's rainy season, came rolling up over the Santiago hills, and each time the sudden darkness was ripped by a lightning flash, the men could still be seen at their work and could be heard roaring out their apostrophe to "The Star Spangled Banner" or putting the best harmonies that they knew to the staccato refrain of "Home Sweet Home."

As these men worked the other men on board

the different vessels of the fleet were called out in obedience to a signal from the flagship that volunteers were wanted, and were told just what was to be done; that no compulsory detail would be made; and that it must be from those willingly offering their services that the Merrimac's last crew would be made up. There had been no attempt to veil the character of the enterprise, in fact it was the policy of the admiral in this case to see that the full gravity of the plan was known all over the fleet.

When the demand for volunteers was therefore made the men knew that they were to steer an undefended, non-combatting ship into the very mouth of Santiago harbor. That no concealment of the vessel's presence was possible or was even contemplated. That every gun guarding Santiago that could be trained upon the Merrimac would be pointed and fired at her. That—for such was the idea then—she would be in point-blank range of the great rapid firing Maxim-Nordenfeldt guns supposed to be at Morro; of the whole of the Socapa battery, of the Hontorias and long bronzes at Punta Gorda, of the guns reputed to be at Cayo Smith—the island which stands at the inner end of the harbor entrance, and of all the cannon, big and little, that were believed to have been placed at every vantage point about the harbor's mouth—that, in fact, she would be the target for more and heavier guns than were trained on Cardigan's light cavalry at Balaklava. They believed that their chances of destruction were in the proportion of one thousand to one of escape; that death was the programme and that escape would be the miracle. They believed that not only did certain annihilation menace them from all around, but that they were to travel to destruction on a vehicle which they themselves had, at the critical instant, to destroy. That if by God's mercy they did get into the channel to that point where it was intended she should lie as a barrier, they were to sink what remained of their craft instantly and effectually, and then to save themselves as best they could by the lifeboat or raft. They believed, granting, still by God's mercy, they had sunk the Merrimac where she should be sunk and had got on board their frail means of escape, that they would be still subjected to the hail of shot from the batteries. They knew and believed all of these things, yet when volunteers were asked for—six were wanted—it was not from twice or even ten times six that the selection had to be made.

Every man in the fleet wanted to go.

In actual figures one hundred and fifty-three

men volunteered from the Iowa, one hundred and forty from the Texas, one hundred and forty-nine from the flagship—men and officers crowding forward and pleading to be allowed a chance not to do or die, but to do and die—so many in literal fact that had all been accepted there would not have been a working crew left on board a single ship.

The men who were selected out of the pushing, crowding, shouting body of volunteers were: gunner's-mate Philip O'Boyle of the Texas; gun-captain Mill of the New Orleans; seaman Anderson of the Massachusetts seaman Wade; of the Vixen; two of the Merrimac's men and Hobson. The Vixen, when the selection had been made, steamed about the fleet picking up the men and then headed for the Merrimac with the double purpose of putting the volunteers on board and taking off the collier's crew.

And here an odd thing came to pass. Commander Miller, of the Merrimac, and the crew of the Merrimac rebelled. They were in charge of the ship they said, and if there was anything to be done with the old craft that was better than slinging coal, any chance of distinguishing themselves, it was but right and fair they should have the benefit of that chance. They could run the Merrimac, they could sink her, and they could die just as well as any one else. It was the insubordination of devotion, the disobedience of heroism. So pertinacious in their determination were the Merrimac's men, indeed, that they would not and did not leave her until the admiral had sent a sharp command to vacate, and then they left growling and swearing at being driven back to the ordinary risks of war.

At midnight Admiral Sampson went on board the Merrimac to inspect the arrangements, said they were excellent, and left with the full intention of having the vessel go in by daybreak that morning, Thursday, June 2. The tide, however, did not exactly serve and the admiral decided to postpone the attempt until the next night. Word was sent to Hobson to this effect, Hobson sending back the message:

"Mr. Hobson's compliments to the admiral, and he requests that he be allowed to make the attempt now, feeling certain that he can succeed."

To this the admiral sent reply, "Wait until to-morrow," and so far as postponement went, that ended it. The plans were not changed, although the postponement brought about a change in the people. Hobson remained, but it was considered by the head judges of character that the first batch of volunteers had undergone too great a strain by the long wait without compensating event, and so they were sent back to their ships as wretched and broken-hearted a set of men as ever had their lives given back to them. Again, came the mustering for volunteers, again, the scenes of enthusiasm, and again, the selection of the little band of volunteers. The octette of immortals were those:

Hobson, of course; George Charette, gunner's-mate of the flagship New York; Osborn Diegnau, coxswain of the Merrimac; George F. Phillips, machinist of the Merrimac; Francis Kelly, water-tender of the Merrimac; Daniel Montague, master-at-arms of the Brooklyn; J. C. Murphy, coxswain of the Iowa; and Randolph Cranson, coxswain of the New York.

Six men only were chosen as before, but Cranson dropped down in the darkness to the Merrimac and hid in the hold. When this remarkable stowaway was discovered it was too late to send him back and he was allowed to stay.

The Merrimac's old officers and men having been sent to the Texas in growling discontent, and the new volunteers being safely on board the collier, she lay alongside the flagship in order to receive final instructions. So that Hobson and his men might be relieved of all work except the great task of running his vessel through the gauntlet of flame and shot, a pilot was detailed to give Hobson the steerway up to the harbor entrance, and a special crew of forty volunteers was sent on board to work her to that point where the pilot was to leave and the Merrimac was to take her final run.

As the afternoon wore on another great thunderstorm came up, but with sunset came a quiet—skies clearing where they had been black and riven by lightning, and seas running smoothly where they had been whipped and torn by the fierce gusts of wind, and the cascades of water that always accompany these sub-tropical summer storms. Hobson came on board the flagship about nightfall to see the admiral. He was in full uniform, but as he had been crawling around through the bulkheads of the collier and personally inspecting the layout of the torpedoes and the unshipping of the sea valves, he was in a condition of grime that passes description. He started to apologize, but the admiral stopped him.

"Every soot spot is a service mark, Mr. Hobson," he said.

Hobson was told that Naval Cadet Joseph Wright Powell, a slip of a fellow from Oswego, N. Y., would follow the Merrimac in the New York's launch and pick them up, on which he turned to the cadet and said:

"Powell, watch the boat's crew when we pull out of the harbor. We will be cracks rowing thirty strokes to the minute."

He had not been told, however, that there had been almost as fierce a fight for the command of the launch as there had been for a position in the Merrimac's forlorn hope; that the contest, which had almost developed into a scrimmage, had narrowed down to an issue between Cadets Palmer and Powell, and that these two had settled the matter by drawing cigarettes from a box, he who drew the last being the man to go. When Hobson in all his grime and in the full knowledge of what he had to face left the admiral to go on board the Merrimac, the officers and men all crowded round to shake him by the hand and wish him a God's blessing. It was noted by those who did get at his hand and who could look closely into his face, that there was not the faintest assumption in his demeanor that he was going to do something great and unusual, but the simple, quiet bearing and the unaffected temperature of a man who had a duty to do and who was not in the habit of letting his duty interfere with his heartbeat.

Night came and with it a moon that silvered the hills around Santiago, but which left the harbor mouth in deep shadow. The fleet withdrew to about six miles from shore forming a crescent, leaving in the center of its arc the Merrimac. When last seen by the fleet's men Hobson was standing on the collier's bridge talking to the pilot. The subsidary crew was at its post and in its usual garb, but Hobson's aspecial men were grouped underneath the bridge and were stripped to their underclothing. Midnight was sounded on the fleet bells, then the first three morning hours, and still no signal from the admiral for the Merrimac to move.

At last, at twenty-five minutes past three of Friday, June 3, the lamp signals to start were run up and the Merrimac began to move. If eyes had been strained to see the last of Hobson, they were strained doubly now to see the last of the Merrimac. It was the pilot's duty to run the collier into such a position that it meant a clear straight-away dash to the harbor entrance, but to the strung senses of the watchers everything appeared to be going wrong, and as though fate were determined to give Hobson and his men every possible wrench. The Merrimac was seen to flutter, as it were, for a moment, and it was thought that she was off her course. Then she was seen again running and then to stop. This time it was made out that she was properly headed and that the pilot and subsidiary crew were leaving her.

So quiet was the night and so still was every one keeping that through her open ports and hatchways could be heard the jingle of the Merrimac's engine-room bell, and as it was heard the smoke was seen to come tumbling out of her funnel as she jumped ahead. Then the fleet saw her no more, for she had entered the great shadows of the harbor hills.

The light of El Morro burned bright but quiet, and as it was not swept over the arc of the entrance the watchers imagined for one wild moment that the Merrimac might have slipped by the forts unobserved, but scarcely had this hope been formed when from out the eastern side there came an arrow of flame, and with this signal flash and following roar, the hills on each side of the harbor became volcanoes.

By Cadet Powell, in charge of the launch, acting as life saver, it was calculated that Hobson had got to within three hundred yards of the entrance before the first shore gun was fired, and to his wrought-up fancy it seemed that not even in a bombardment from the fleet had he seen such a screaming, flashing, continuous fire as that which followed the Spanish gunner's discovery of the Merrimac.

Certainly the water about the collier was white with foam as though it had been whipped with a hail storm, while to the plunging fire of the batteries was added the continuous rattle of the garrison's musketry. Powell held it to be absolutely impossible for the Merrimac even to advance in the face of such a reception, much less live, but on she plowed through it all until, just as she had been lost to the view of the fleet in the shadow of the cliffs, so, she was lost to Powell's view as she dashed in between them.

Then above the scream and roar of the guns and the snap and whistle of the rifles came five thunder claps that drowned all the Spaniard's noise and the fleet knew either that she had been blown up by mines, or at least, one man had lived through it all and had touched off the battery.

Then a silence where there had been such an uproar and nothing seen until a quarter past five, when Powell's launch was discovered steaming out from the shore followed by a new clatter and shrieking from the Spanish forts as they picked up this little craft and did their best to blow her into matchwood. But she raced safely to the shelter of the flagship's drab sides, although it was to bring the sad report that "No one had come out of the entrance to the harbor." No one had supposed that Powell would save a single member of the Merrimac's men or that any one would be left to save. So Powell's report was simply looked on as one of the incidents in the inevitable catastrophe.

But no, Hobson had not only measurably done what he started to do, he had done it without losing a man, and almost without a scratch. Riddled like a sieve as she was he had pushed the Merrimac past the forts, over the mines, two of which exploded, and had driven her staggering right to the selected spot and then, while shot and shell plowed and plunged about them, each man had done his particular duty as though fear or haste, or need to haste were unknown quantities.

The anchor lines were cut, the two anchors flew down bringing the ship up with a jerk as their flukes caught below, and then, as the tide swung her round in the channel, the valves were opened, engines stopped, and with three bellowing crashes and three rending staggering blows at her sides, that number of torpedoes was exploded and the Merrimac settled in ninety seconds and in thirty feet of water.

The whaleboat had been blown to pieces but the catamaran was saved, and on this Hobson and his men leaped just before the ship began to settle. There was no chance for them to get into the open sea and so Hobson, characteristically, decided to make for the Spanish shore. As the

Spanish gunners saw the raft put off from the sinking hulk they forbore to fire, and when the men reached shore the Spanish gunners shook hands with them and patted them on the back. And when they were marched as prisoners to Cervera, the Spanish admiral not only shook hands with them and patted them on the back, but embraced the quiet Alabamian and told him that he was a man after his own heart.

More than this, he sent Captain Oviedo, his chief of staff, out to Admiral Sampson with a flag of truce and a long message of compliments, a report of what had been accomplished, all done as an act of appreciation shown by one sailor to another sailor concerning the brave act of still another sailor.

And so it was learned that what Hobson had started out to do he had done. He had done it with nothing more than the hope that he might be allowed to live long enough to sink his ship, but to him and to the brave men who were with him there had come that sheltering hand that seems always extended over those who, with clear heads and calm souls, go steadfastly along their lines of duty.

Neither the entities of history nor of narrative will be destroyed if it is told here how "with weeping and with laughter" Hobson and his fellow heroes came into the American lines July 6. It had been supposed, in view of Admiral Cervera's extreme courteousness toward the constructor, that an exchange of the Merrimac's men might easily be effected. Such was not the case, however, and after dallying negotiations which were carried limpingly around the circle from Blanco to Washington, and from Washington to Madrid, from Madrid to Santiago and thence to Havana again, the matter came to a standstill.

It happened, however, that at the battle of El Caney we had captured, among many others, a Lieutenant Arios, of the aristocratic Barcelona regiment, and with Arios and his fellow-officers in our hands we were able effectually to treat for an exchange. On the morning of July 6, a meeting took place under a tree midway between the lines of the Rough Riders and those of the first Spanish intrenchments. Colonel John Jacob Astor conducted to this rendezvous three Lieutenants Volez, Aurolius, and Arios, besides fourteen sergeants, corporals and privates. Hobson and his men came out under charge of Major Iries, a Spanish staff officer. The Spanish prisoners were kept blindfolded until they reached the point of exchange; the eyes of the American prisoners were unbandaged. Iries was told that he might have all fourteen of the men and his choice of the officers. Without hesitation he chose the aristocrat. Then Colonel Astor put out his hand to Hobson saying:

"My name is Astor, and I'm mighty glad to welcome you back to freedom."

"Thank you, colonel," replied the Alabamian, "if you are half as glad as I am to get back, there is no question as to the warmth of your welcome."

Then the Spanish major and the American colonel looked at their watches, and seeing that the hour of truce, during which this little pacific interlude had been conducted, was on the point of expiring, bowed with Americo-Castilian politeness to each other and went back to their lines.

If Hobson had been of the stuff that is puffed into bullfrog uselessness he would surely have been spoiled by the reception which his fighting compatriots accorded him from the first intrenchment to the last vessel of the fleet. The Rough Riders, cowboys and college men, swarmed out of the trenches and over the guns yelling like Comanches; swept them off their feet and bore them on their shoulders inside the lines. Then the colored troopers swarmed about and the Alabama white shook hands with the Georgia black as though slave days had ended five centuries ago;

every soldier who knew what was going on yelled as though he had personally secured freedom from a Spanish cell; the wounded in the hospital at Siboney sat up in their cots and cheered, and when the launch bearing the released prisoners put off from Daiquiri in the dusk of the evening and made for the New York, every ship's whistle tooted and every ship's men cheered, and even Admiral Sampson stepped over his habitual reserve and embraced Hobson with almost as much effusion as had the Spanish admiral.

Hobson's story, a characteristically simple one, cleared up many points that had been in doubt. He said that he and his associates had been confined in Morro Castle but four days, being removed thence on board the Reina Mercedes which the Spanish were using as a hospital ship. The kind greeting which Cervera had granted them bore its fruit and during the whole thirty-three days of their incarceration their treatment by the Spanish was most courteous.

It was not a keen sighted gunner, as had been supposed, who first caught a glimpse of the Merrimac stealing into Santiago, but a patrol boat which ran close up under the stern of the Merrimac and fired several shots at her from a three-pounder. In this fire the Merrimac's rudder was carried away. The picket boat at once gave the alarm and in a moment the guns of the Vizcaya, Almirante Oquendo and shore batteries were turned upon the collier, while sub-marine mines and torpedoes grumbled and exploded all about her.

When the Merrimac was in the desired position and the attempt was made to throw her across the channel the loss of the rudder was discovered. It was not possible therefore, to do this, but the anchors were thrown out and the tide swung her so that she blocked the passageway for some three-quarters of it. As the anchors were dropped the catamaran was launched and Hobson touched off the battery. At that same moment two torpedoes, fired by the Reina Mercedes, struck the Merrimac amidships and in the combined shock the collier was lifted out of the water and almost rent asunder.

It is worthy of remark that one of the first acts of Hobson after his return to the New York was a request to the admiral that he might be allowed to take a battleship into the harbor, claiming that the shore fortifications were not nearly as formidable as was supposed. Quite as characteristically, Sampson concluded that his policy of long distance bombardment was better **than the constructor's** plan of venture and dash.

CHAPTER III.

HOW THE MARINES FOUGHT AT GUANTANAMO.

The whole campaign at Santiago was so full of spectacular effects and valiant deeds, done individually and collectively, that what would under ordinary circumstances mark an epoch, becomes but an incident in the revival of America's military spirit. Treading close on the heels of Hobson's exploit, for instance, came Huntington's defense of Fisherman's Point at Guantanamo Bay, leading up to the first battle on Cuban soil, and of which some future historian will make a book.

With Cervera at Santiago, the seat of war in the West Indies, as has been said, was suddenly and distinctively removed to that port. It meant the determination to destroy the Spanish admiral's fleet together with the city's investment by sea and land, and our government at once set to work to dispatch the beleaguering forces southward. But the mobilization and transport of an invading army, especially when that army is to enter on a tropical campaign and has been raised from the basis of a citizen soldiery, is a task whose rapid and successful accomplishment should mean the canonization of the quartermaster-general. In every such enterprise some bureau, some group of men, is sure to be ahead of the others—to form a sort of process on the body military, so to speak. In this case it was Lieutenant Colonel Robert W. Huntington and his six hundred marines, who for weeks had been cramped and packed on the sweltering decks of the troop ship Panther off Tampa, before her commander received instructions to weigh anchor and report to Sampson off Santiago.

It was at ten o'clock on Friday morning, June 10, that the troop ship under convoy of the Yosemite steamed up to the blockading fleet and half an hour later she had put about for Guantanamo to land her marines. The place had been selected as a base of operations and supplies, and, topographically it was an ideal selection. The harbor of Guantanamo is one of the best on the south coast of Cuba. It lies thirty-eight miles east of Santiago, the town and fort being situated about five miles back from the coast. There are no established fortifications to speak of at the entrance to the harbor, but prior to the arrival of the Panther's men, the Spaniards—who kept

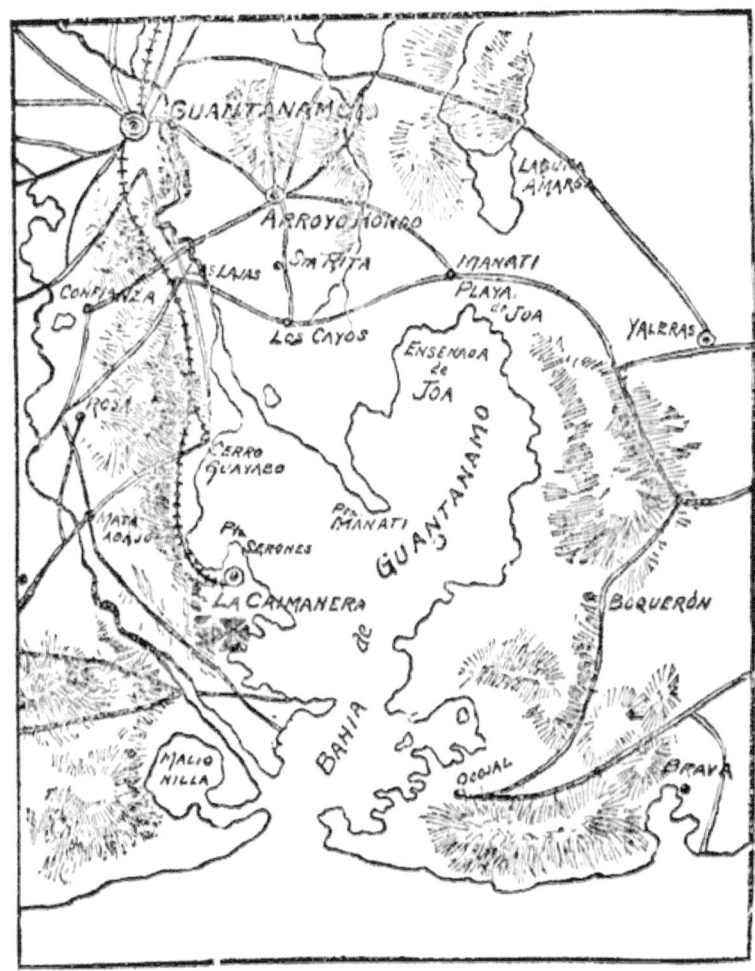

Guantanamo Bay and its surrounding—Where Huntington's marines established the first United States military camp in Cuba.

singularly well informed as to our intended movements—had thrown up earthworks and dug rifle pits from which to command this entrance. Here, in order to understand what follows, it will be necessary to gain as clear an idea as possible of the lay of the land.

Looking shoreward from on board ship you would see to the west, that is to the left of the entrance, a rather extensive strip of low lying, swampy ground. To the right is a sandy stretch covered with bushes and cacti from which rises the shoulder of a range of steep, almost precipitous, rocky hills running parallel with the shore and ending in a lagoon. Up and down the face of the hills are jutting rocks and patches of faded vegetation, while at their base on the little rocky ledge or beach is, or was, a straggling collection of fishermen's huts, one or two stores, and the distinctively clean looking cable office. Between the swampy lowland of the west and the clifflike hills of the east lay spread out the curving waterway into Guantanamo harbor. On the bare, brown summit of a bluff which formed a step of the cliff and in caves in the cliff itself, the Spaniards had placed their earthworks and rifle pits and out of these earthworks and rifle pits, Captain McCalla had driven them on the day before with the guns of the Marblehead.

If you landed and toiled up one of the steep zig-zag trails until you stood on the top of the bluff beside the deserted earthworks and looked inland you would see that the shore mountains really comprised three distinct, heavily-wooded ranges of a gradually increasing elevation and with equally heavily-wooded gullies between the ridges. Back of the ridges stretched out the flat lands around the upper end of the bay on which it set down the city of Guantanamo. Looking across the bay you would see the village and fort of Caimanera and the railroad running up to Guantanamo.

When the Panther reached Guantanamo bay the fishing village and its defenses were found to be deserted alike by fishermen and soldiers. The marines were all landed, in quick and easy order, running and cheering and stretching their legs like a lot of schoolboys at recess. Then they lugged their equipage up the trails to the breezy bluff, where they pitched their tents, established camp and named it after the commander of the Marblehead. The Spaniards had left a flagpole and just before sunset, while the shore detail was burning up the wretched little village below, as the most convenient form of fumigating the locality, the Stars and Stripes were run up at Camp McCalla, the main body of marines was drawn up in line and the first establishment of United States troops on Cuban soil was greeted with cheers from above and below, and by a salute from the little fleet lying in the roadstead. Then the men sang and ate and frolicked and at ten o'clock the camp, save for the sentries, was as quiet as a wood in winter.

The quiet lasted just two hours, for everybody agreed that it was midnight, when, instead of six hundred sleeping men there were six hundred swearing marines startled into half-wakefulness by a shot, a sentry's challenge and then a cracking volley. If the first moment was one of half-wakefulness, the second was one of complete activity, and in two minutes the rifles of the marines were all vigorously replying to the crack and splutter of the Spanish Mausers that came, or seemed to come from the chaparral-covered slopes to the east. The long Mauser bullets were singing over the marines' heads, but no one was hit and as the hail from the Lees battered the brush which concealed the Spaniards, the firing from the thicket soon lessened.

It did not, however, cease and all that night Huntington's men were kept awake and on the jump by single shots and volleys from the guerrillas. Neither was there any rest for the marines during daylight on Saturday. The volley firing ceased, it is true, but the camp was made the center for one of the most aggravating and nerve-destroying forms of attack of which it is possible to conceive.

Untried, absolutely inexperienced in any form of land fighting, all the marines had to fall back on was the discipline of drill and individual grit. But in no tactics had they ever come across anything that met the exigencies of the present occasion. Nearly all town-bred, conscious that at all times they were regarded as a sort of marine police, they found themselves suddenly called on to bear the brunt of an attack so harassing and unusual that to meet it would have called up all the experience and cunning of our plain and lava-bed fighters. Instead of fighting the Spanish troops in Cuba the Panther's men might really have been fighting the Sioux in the Bad Lands of South Dakota. Like the half-blind man in the Bible they saw men as trees walking, for the Spaniards, stripping themselves to the buff reclothed themselves with the Adamic garb of leaves, and, gently waving palm trees over their heads, crept stealthily here and there until a tongue of fire and a singing bullet showed that instead of a piece of tropical vegetation it was a Spanish sharp-shooter. Not only were the Spaniards masked but they were, undoubtedly, **under** the very prince of guerrilla fighters; one who, to the cunning of the Indian added the cruelty of the Inquisitorial Spaniard. Silenced at one point, the bushwhackers would break out into furious firing from another; then, when all the bush seemed to have been battered into silence by the marines, the rifle fire would blaze out from a hundred points at once.

Although under this scattering but persistent fire from the Spaniards all day, Huntington kept his men at work strengthening the earthworks, digging new rifle pits, and dragging up the battalion's field-pieces from the beach, and when Saturday night came the marines were ready enough to bless their commander for his prescience and discipline. Sleep was absolutely out of the question. All through the night, shadowy figures could be dimly seen creeping through the edge of the bush that rose around the camp. There was the constant, tense, singing note of the Mauser balls following the sharp pop of the Spanish rifles; the humming deeper note of the Lee bullets following the louder ring of the marines' weapons; while, as the result of a counsel between Huntington, Philip and McCalla, the Texas and Marblehead added their deeper note to the serenade. The warships swung their searchlights on to the bush, and sent in their launches with orders to let fly their howitzers at any illuminated spot that showed a Spaniard as a blot in its cone of light.

It was all decidedly picturesque, but neither the searchlights nor the howitzers of the launches, nor the constant blazing of the marines at anything that seemed to suspiciously move in the undergrowth brought any relief to Camp McCalla. As a desperate resort a detail of men was sent out to set fire to the jungle, but this proved impossible on account of the lush young trees which formed the undergrowth. While the attempt was being made to smoke out the guerrillas from the nearest slope, the Spaniards appeared in the bush across the lagoon to the east of the camp. They were driven thence by the searchlights of the Marblehead and the clever drop of a few screeching shells only to appear in a ravine on the east side near the bay shore. And so it went on all night, until from want of sleep, because of the long fight with shadows, and from a night of noise unspeakable the men, when daylight struck them, looked as haggard as though they had camped for a fortnight in a stable of nightmares.

There had been men killed, too. Not many, it is true, not one per cent of what would have been the result had the Spaniards' aim approached in accuracy the cleverness of their tactics. Those who had been killed and wounded had been shot down almost at the rifle's muzzle, and so horrible were the effects of the fierce wire nails of the Mausers at this distance that it was supposed at first the Spaniards had been guilty of unutterable mutilations.

For the first time our surgeons were able to make a close study of what a Mauser rifle-shot wound was like. To their reports the curious student of the horrors of modern warfare is referred. All that need be said here is that the dead and wounded in the fighting around Guantanamo bay showed that the Mauser bullet when received at close range makes at its point of entrance only a small hole, but at its point of exit it seems to take everything with it. In size the bullet is as the section of an ordinary lead pencil one and a half inches long. It is nickel covered, but while the charges of mutilation, which Admiral Sampson laid against the Spaniards when he saw the dreadful character of the men's wounds, were withdrawn, the evidence would seem to show that in some cases the nickel points of the bullets had been scraped away. The result was that the exposed lead mushroomed on its impact and when to this spreading quality of the missile was added its rotary motion, the resulting wound, as may be imagined, was a frightful one. Those killed at Guantanamo and struck in the head would have been scarcely more shattered had they stood in the path of a shell.

The marines saw these things, and they saw, too, that their camp on the bluff, breezy though it might be, was, on account of the thickly wooded hills around it and its own bareness, little more than a target for the Spanish bushwhackers. Huntington saw this also, and when Sunday morning came he decided to move camp to the landing-place on Fisherman's Point. McCalla sent sixty-five Cuban insurgents, and Philip added a squad of bluejackets and two Colt automatic guns to assist in the moving. Instead of being a day of rest it was a day of din, distress and desperation. The Spaniards swarmed through the bushes and every move made by the marines was under a hot fire. In the midst of it those who had been killed, including Assistant Surgeon Gibbs, had to be buried, but the same spirit that prompted the scraping of the Mauser bullet and the shooting of a noncombatant under the shadow of the Red Cross stood out ferociously even here.

Graves were dug in the red, stony soil of the bluff to the north of the camp and a squad of marines was sent ashore from the Texas to act as

Graves of Acting Assistant Surgeon John B. Gibbs, Private William Dumphy, and Private J. McColgan, killed on the hill, Guantanamo Bay, June 11, 1898.

funeral escort, Huntington's marines being too busy in the diverse labors of moving camp and potting the Spanish bushwhackers. About the time the little procession, headed by Chaplain Jones of the Texas, had stumbled over the rocky ground to the improvised graveyard, the firing from the bush slackened sufficiently for the men of Camp McCalla to look around. They saw this little procession, and laying down their Lees in the trenches, stepped over and fell in after the Texas men. No sooner had they done this than the skulking Spaniards turned a hot fire on the funeral party. For a moment or two chaplain, escort, and marines paid no attention to the fusillade, but grouped themselves about the open graves, the chaplain, it is true, stepping behind the mounds of new turned earth, but without dropping a word of the service. The sad little ceremony would have been concluded with this attendance had not the Spaniards crept in force up to the nearest clumps of bushes from which the bullets were so persistently whistled that chaplain, mourners and corpses alike seemed in danger of being riddled.

This was too much for the men of Camp McCalla, and with a cry of "Fall in," they rushed for their rifles in the trenches. As they broke away from the funeral they had begun the intoning of the Lord's Prayer, and it was without ceasing the full-throated intercession that, throwing themselves flat, they pegged fiercely away at the hidden and pitiless enemy. The pump of the Lee bullets was as rhythmical as the intoned phrases. It was a prayer punctuated with gunshots, and was only another instance of the Puritan spirit—the spirit of the Bible and sword carried hand to hand into battle—that marked this whole campaign. The ships in the bay sniffed the contest from afar and turned loose their shells and machine guns, and it was to this martial accompaniment that the dead were buried, Chaplain Jones committing his brethren to the ground without a break in his sonorous voice, and without a cringe in his long, thin form as he stood full in the strong sunlight.

Although the camp was moved to the beach, the intrenchments on the hilltop were not deserted. The American flag had been planted on the site of the destroyed blockhouse, and it was not to be taken down or forsaken. New trenches were dug and the defending guns better placed. Still the attacks from the bush were maintained, varied now by dashes on the beach camp from the chaparral growing around the eastern lagoon. More men were killed and the constant drag and strain were visibly telling on the marines. It was very evident that something had to be done to break this dreadful monotony of fighting hidden foes. A retreat was out of the question, and so it was decided to make at once a sortie and a round up.

How strong the Spaniards might be was not known, the Cuban scouts bringing in estimates that varied from two hundred to two thousand, but it was known that constant accessions to the army of bushwhackers were being ferried across the bay from Caimanera, and that unless some bold movement were made the first American garrison in Cuba stood a very good chance of being shot out of existence or driven into the sea.

Roughly speaking, the Spaniards held the three ranges of hills, before alluded to, and which were like three fingers with two deep valleys between, like the hollows between the fingers. On the first ridge stood a heliograph station; on a mound commanding the first and second ridges stood a blockhouse; and between the second and third ridges was a well, or water tank, around which had been established the guerrilla headquarters. All three, heliograph station, blockhouse, and well, were to be the objects of attack, for it was argued that with their signal station, their stronghold, and their water supply gone, the bushwhackers would find themselves deprived of their three mainstays.

That the enterprise might prove a failure never entered the heads of Huntington and his officers. The woods had to be purged of the Spaniards. That was the simple programme.

Early on Tuesday morning, June 14, two hundred and eighty-nine Americans, and forty-one Cubans were drawn up at Fisherman's Point ready for the desperate expedition. The men were divided into four companies. Captains Elliott and Spicer each had ninety marines and fifteen Cubans in his party. Lieutenants Mahoney and Ingate each had fifty marines in his command, Mahoney having ten Cubans and Ingate one, this latter to act as guide. The Ingate party can be very briefly disposed of. Its contemplated share in the operations was to skirt the first range of hills eastward until it came to the lagoon and then turn northward, that is inland way, so as to be able to attack the guerrilla headquarters from the flank while the other parties were attacking it from the front. Long before the flank movement could be executed, however, Ingate grew suspicious of his Cuban guide and turned back. Elliott and Spicer were to make objectively for the Spanish headquarters, while Mahoney's line of advance was between that of these two captains and that of Ingate, with the capture of the heliograph station and blockhouse as a preliminary duty. The Cubans were to act as scouts and bush-beaters.

The marines were inspected as scrutinizingly as though they were to parade; the Cubans hopped spasmodically about without any semblance of order or preparation. The marines were clad in their brown uniforms, as speckless as though just from the factory; the Cubans wore what the sailors had given them, what rags they had owned, or nothing, as the fancy suited them. The faces of the marines were drawn, bronzed, rather wistful and decidedly determined; those of the Cubans were mostly black and were agleam with satisfaction and pride at having a chance to show the Americans what they could do in fighting the Spanish.

There was a sharp call of order and then the lines of brown, white and black men began to climb up the steep tangled sides of the first ridge. Mahoney's men were first at work. They found the heliograph station guarded by a company of Spaniards and there was immediately the song in unison of Lee and Mauser. The Spaniards had been waiting the attack while the marines had been toiling through the tangle of woods under a broiling sun, but when within shooting range our men went to work at once as steadily and sturdily as though they had been the waiting party. Fifteen minutes of this brisk, deadly work and the Spaniards fled helter-skelter down the inland slope of the first range, where they were joined by the fleeing garrison of the blockhouse, while the marines knelt along the ridge and picked off the fleeing men as they ran or dodged from bush to bush.

Meanwhile Elliott and Spicer's men to the west but moving northward had crossed the first ridge, tramped across the gully, and climbed to the top of the second ridge under a spattering but wild fire of the Spaniards who were stationed here. When our men reached the summit of the second ridge the sun was blazing at high noon, the water in their canteens was a sickly warm fluid and the jungle through which they had come was so full of thorny cactus and tearing mesquite that each step was a struggle. Yet when our men reached this crest and saw the guerrilla headquarters in the valley beneath, a new spirit of freshness took possession of them.

Plainly in view, in the valley before them were the huts of the men, the officer's quarters and the water tank which they had set out to destroy. The marines and Cubans had scrambled up the

ridge on which they now stood in single order
and as best they might, but when once there the
hundred and eighty marines and the thirty
Cubans were formed in line along the crest, with
the Cubans on the left flank and then began to
slowly work their way down, firing as they went.
The long brown and white line moved steadily
down the slope, aiming and firing as it moved,
with the Spaniards' bullets whistling viciously
all about it. The guerrillas fired from the shelter
of the huts and other buildings so that they really
had the advantage of an intrenched position, but
the marines never wavered in their advance.

Now they were at the base of the hill and the
order was given to fix bayonets and charge across
the gully. The gleam and click of the bayonets
were too much for the Spaniards, and in a panic
they left the shelter of the headquarters and
made for the cover of the brush-clad slopes of
the third ridge. Between the huts and brush,
however, there was a clear space of about one
hundred yards, and as the Spaniards galloped
across this open space it was easy shooting for
our men. Still in line they advanced, pouring a
deadly fire into the guerrillas, while the Cubans
waved their machetes and sprang forward with a
howl. Still in line, the brown-clad marines
made straight for the thickets into which the

Spaniards had fled, while the white and black clad Cubans ran and fired, and cursed as they ran. Out of the thickets the Spaniards darted, and as they darted the marines shot them down. Up the slopes the Spaniards climbed and struggled, while the marines climbed and struggled after them and fired as they climbed. Clear to the crest the Spaniards were driven, and then to their dismay another fighting force of these terrible Americans was met.

After capturing the heliograph station and blockhouse Mahoney and his men had skirted the eastern end of the second and third ridges in anticipation of just what was happening so that when the terror-stricken Spaniards started to scamper down this third ridge Mahoney's fifty marines and ten Cubans were waiting for them. Back the Spaniards ran and as they scrambled once more on to the crest of the third ridge, still another enemy appeared. Huntington had taken counsel with the commander of the Dolphin, and that gunboat had been watching all the morning for just this opportunity. With their glasses the Dolphin's officers had been sweeping the hills for a good chance for a long shot and when the Spaniards appeared crowding the hilltop they knew they had that chance. Down dropped the shells in the midst of the dismayed Spaniards and again they rushed to the hillside. Again, Mahoney's men met them and as the Spaniards turned back again they were met by Captain Elliott's marines moving steadily up the slope and by the fierce assault of the Cubans.

Three times over that terrible ridge were the Spanish guerrillas thus driven. With two musketry cross-fires, the assaults of the Cubans and the bursting of the shells as a composite horror, the Spaniards finally made their disordered way down the further side of the last ridge and so into the shelter of the Guantanamo lowlands. The five days of persistent cruel bush attacks had been amply revenged. In the sortie two Cubans had been killed and one of our marines wounded, while of the Spanish some one hundred killed and wounded lay between the heliograph station and the last slope of the third ridge. To wind up the expedition the water tank and headquarters were destroyed, the blockhouse razed, eighteen prisoners captured, and a hundred rifles and a thousand rounds of ammunition brought back by the dripping, wearied, but triumphant, little army.

It was not a very great affair, but barring the funny little Gussie expedition it was the first battle on Cuban soil between American and Spanish forces. Moreover, it was a fight between unseasoned, wearied men, fighting their way through an enemy's country, and a much superior force of seasoned veterans holding a strong position. The odds had been all against us, but the honors were all ours. From Spanish sources it was afterward learned that the defenders of the hills included at least two companies of picked regulars and two companies of guerrillas, numbering in all four hundred and eighty men. The actual losses on the Spanish sides in the six days fighting cannot be stated, but they were approximately one hundred and fifty killed and wounded, while ours were five killed and fifteen wounded.

Having driven the bushwhackers off the ridges and destroyed their rallying center, it was next decided to put a stop to the constant accession of reinforcements which had been received by the bushwhackers from Guantanamo by way of Caimanera. Every day new detachments of Spanish soldiers had been brought from the city by railroad to the fort and earthworks, and these it was decided to reduce. Accordingly on the day following the successful sweep of the marines over the hills, the Texas, Marblehead and Suwanee sailed into Guantanamo Bay, and from two until half-past three o'clock in the afternoon rained shells on the brickwork and intrench-

The Marines at Guantanamo as they fell in preparatory to driving the guerillas out of the bush.

ments. At the end of this bombardment the fort was a brick pile and the trenches were little more than reddish-brown dirt heaps, while the garrison, or such as was left of it, had taken train to Guantanamo.

The infliction of these two blows taught the Spaniards their lesson, and from that time on the outer bay of Guantanamo and the hills overlooking Fisherman's Point were as placid and untroubled as a summer resort. A varying number of colliers lay at anchor within Fisherman's Point, the Panther was anchored close beside the camp, the Solace rode in the smooth sheltered waters of the bay, the Marblehead, as flagship of the station, steamed here and there, the cable office was re-established and officially known as Pleya del Este, vessels from the blockading squadron came and went, rowboats and launches moved rapidly about, no Spaniard was to be seen, and that which was the theater of a seven-days' continuous performance of unrest, distress and bloodshed became so peaceful that the captured Spaniard's letter dolefully describing the American occupation of Guantanamo Bay as the matter of fact conversion of the place into "a harbor of rest" exactly fitted the transformation.

CHAPTER IV.

HOW SHAFTER LANDED HIS ARMY AT DAIQUIRI.

When Huntington's marines were landed at Guantanamo Bay it was in the expectation that the army of investment would reach Santiago almost immediately thereafter. It was three weeks, however, before the transports, with their fifteen thousand and odd American soldiers, were sighted by the blockading fleet.

Major-General William Rufus Shafter, in command of the Fifth Army Corps, had been selected to lead the army of invasion, and Tampa was chosen as the point of debarkation. As has been intimated, the dispatch of an army largely composed of unseasoned men is a task that might try the capabilities of a quartermaster's department accustomed to the active operations at home and abroad of an enormous standing army; but when it meant the sudden call upon a department used only to the gentle and easy demands of a tiny standing army accustomed only to garrison life and police duties on the plains, it became a matter whose exactions can scarcely be measured.

The Fall of Santiago. 73

The invading army consisted of the following forces:

INFANTRY—		
Officers............................	561	
Enlisted men....................	10,709	
		11,270
CAVALRY (Dismounted)—		
Officers............................	168	
Enlisted men....................	3,155	
		3,323
ARTILLERY—		
Officers............................	18	
Enlisted men....................	455	
		473
ENGINEERS—		
Officers............................	9	
Enlisted men....................	200	
		209
SIGNAL CORPS		15
		15,290
TOTAL FIGHTING MEN—		
Officers............................	747	
Enlisted men....................	14,319	
		15,066
Fieldpieces......................................		24
Horses...		578
Mules..		1,301

For three weeks things at Tampa were chaotic. The water supply was short; machinery broke down; siege guns had to be carried bodily for miles; embarkation stages had to be built; supply trains were stalled; mules and horses that should have arrived had been left behind in some unknown locality; troops were coming in from a dozen different camps in a dozen different stages of unpreparedness—such were a few of the tangles, drawbacks and difficulties which had to be met, unraveled, and conquered before the great transport fleet could get on her way.

Every one, from Shafter down, was in a feverish condition of fume and fret. The war fury of the soldiers was rapidly changing into one of weariness and disgust, while the foreign representatives who peered everywhere and watched everything, confided to their respective governments that the army of invasion was an armed mob and that the quartermaster's department had gone to pieces. As a plain matter of fact, the work done in the way of licking raw material into shape, and in the arming, equipping, and forwarding of Shafter's army compared most favorably with anything done in the same line by nations who are adepts in the art of war. It was May 29 when Schley's dispatch was received saying that Cervera was in Santiago harbor, and it was on the 14th of June that the army for Santiago sailed from Tampa, an interval of only sixteen days in which inventive spirit, Yankee push, and the indomitable conquest of obstacles had done all that could have been accomplished by the practiced military experts and well-oiled war bureaus of Europe.

There was impatience everywhere, of course; in the press, at headquarters in Washington, and with the blockading fleet. Every day the lookouts off Santiago watched for the smoke of the transport armada coming around Cape Maysi, and as each day closed with the report that there was nothing in sight, that impatience grew. Upon Admiral Sampson devolved not only the duty of preventing the escape of Cervera's fleet, but also that of preventing if possible the junction of the various divisions of the Spanish army which were known to be scattered up and down the eastern end of the island and which he was sure would be making every effort to effect a concentration in Santiago city. Envoys were sent to General Calixto Garcia, asking him to move his forces of insurgents down to the southern coast so as to hold if possible the passes leading from Manzanillo and Holquin through which the various Spanish garrisons would have to come. To this Garcia replied by sending General Rabi to the north of Santiago with nine hundred men, and six hundred, under Castillo, to the east of the city, while he, Garcia, established his headquarters at Aceraderos, fourteen miles west of Santiago, to await the arrival of the American troops. As further and useful ways of passing the waiting time, there was more cable cutting and another striking attention was given to the forts guarding the entrance to Santiago harbor. There were several small exchanges with the forts, but the only two of consequence, in addition to that which they received at the hands of Schley soon after his arrival, were the bombardments of the forts by the entire blockading fleet, which took place on the 6th and 16th of June.

The endeavors to reduce the harbor fortifications on these two dates were valuable as lessons and practice, but so far as the reduction of the forts went they were practically without result. We learned again at Santiago what the allied forces had learned at Sebastopol and Cronstadt, and what we had learned at Charleston. When the shells fell unpleasantly near the gunners they left their guns, and when the bombardment was over the damages were repaired and the forts and batteries were in as good fighting trim as before. During these two bombardments our ships expended ammunition to the value of three hundred thousand dollars, killed and wounded less than three hundred Spaniards, and at the conclusion of the engagements Morro was practically unscathed and the earthworks practically as good as ever.

Nor did these bombardments result in drawing a very heavy Spanish fire, the return from all

the fortifications being extremely small and deliberate. Not more than ten per cent. of the guns in place was used, and if our attacks were practically without result the Spanish reply was absolutely unproductive of harm.

Neither can the bombardment by the dynamite cruiser or gunboat Vesuvius be said to have effected the "tremendous revolution in naval warfare" which some people expected of her. The first use of the Vesuvius was on Monday, June 13. Commander Pillsbury had been begging Sampson ever since his arrival off Santiago for permission to try his three pneumatic tubes, and on Monday night he gained the admiral's consent. It was dark as a pit's mouth all about the harbor entrance, and under cover of this blackness the Vesuvius crept up to within three-quarters of a mile and fired her first gun.

The term is used only as a colloquialism, for as one of description it is entirely inaccurate. When the Vesuvius discharged her shell there was no smoke, no flash and, in place of an explosion, a peculiar husky, wheezing sound, as though—so said the sailors in homely but expressive phrase—some gigantic cow had been choked with an enormous turnip and were trying to cough it up. But, while the emission and flight of the projectile—a contact exploding shell containing two hundred pounds of gun cotton—were noiseless, the landing of the missile was thunderous. Three shells at this time were fired, all three exploded on impact and each explosion was as though there had been some convulsion of nature—not so much a deafening sound as an all-pervading and appalling concussion.

Here again, while it was proved that the Vesuvius could successfully discharge her gun-cotton shells, that these shells would traverse a great distance, that impact meant detonation, and that detonation meant a convulsion of the countryside—this practically limited the accomplishment of her bombardment. It was found afterward—and following other bombardments—that where the shells struck they changed the topography of the coast, and that the demoralizing effect of a silently emitted shell that shook the hills and plowed up the valleys when it struck home was very great, but it was also found that the fact of the vessel's being her own gun-carriage and the fixed elevation of the tubes meant that it was almost impossible to aim accurately at a fortified eminence. The Vesuvius where her tubes could be brought to bear on an extended area, well in range, and chiefly within the limited parabola of her shells' flight, would doubtless be a tremendous engine of destructiveness, but the fact remains that she did not tear up a single fort off Santiago nor send a single gun flying into space.

Meanwhile the armada of invasion was being rushed into sailing form, and at last the final rendezvous of the fleet was made just inside the bar at the mouth of Tampa Bay at 3:50 P.M. June 14, and two hours later it got under way. The mobilization of the transport fleet had been accomplished with much shuttle work between the various points of rendezvous, but when it had formed into fair sailing order and was steaming across the waters of the gulf it formed a naval pageant whose like had not been seen since the days of Philip of Spain and Drake.

Stretching over twenty miles of sea and moving slowly ahead at a seven-knot rate the great fleet advanced in three parallel columns. In number they were forty; in formation the transports kept in triple column, preceded and flanked by the armed convoys. At the head of the central column of transports steamed the Detroit with pennant flying; while to the right of the troop ships were aligned the Indiana, Annapolis, Castine and Panther. In patrol duty the Bancroft flitted along to the left; the Hornet and Scorpion steamed in among the troop ships like marshals at a parade to keep the procession well in order, while the Helena brought up the rear. As in a procession, too, sometimes the divisions would become ill spaced. Then the whole parade would halt and the little steaming, puffing marshals would scurry here and there, driving the laggard into place or keeping back too restive a member, while the transport steamers marked time by rolling and pitching in the short running seas. All around, like the uneasy boys on the street flitted the press dispatch boats and private craft attracted by the novelty, danger and excitement of the event.

Guarded, though it was, by warships and moving though it might be into the enemy's waters, there was nothing about the whole fleet that would indicate impending fight. It was, rather, the ostentatious, open order of a floating armament devised as a spectacle. Far as the eye could reach the ships spread out covering the sea, as open to the enemy's view as though it had been a moving continent. The guns of the great pyramidical Indiana boomed out a salute to the commanding general, the Bancroft howled orders through her siren, and so vast was the formation that had an enemy attacked the rear the Indiana could not have seen it even from her fighting tops.

The Fall of Santiago.

There was a bright sunshine, sky and sea were both of the vividest blue, and over sky and sea both there rushed white flecks—these of clouds, those of foam. The decks of the ships were crowded with men; right at the head of the middle column flew a dark-blue flag with its Maltese cross at the foremast head of the Saguranca, the headquarters of General Shafter; orders were shouted here and there through the megaphone; the hospital ship steamed about like a doctor on his visits inquiring the health of his patients in reply to the sick signal, and so with running seas, bright skies by day and lighted ships by night the great armada moved majestically along.

On Friday, June 17, those on the transport fleet caught the first sight of the Cuban coast, a white lighthouse on the outlying key of Paredon Grande. Then on Saturday the mainland came into view—hazy hills along Cape Lucretia; Sunday morning the fleet turned into the Windward Passage; Cape Maysi was rounded at night, and early on the morning of Monday, June 21, the seventh day of the fleet's journey from Port Tampa, the great broken Sierras that lie around Santiago came into view.

As an evidence of the impatience with which the arrival of the transport fleet had been awaited, the two tugs, Resolute and Wompatuck, were seen by the lookout men on board the Indiana steaming about Cape Maysi like pilots on the lookout for a patron, and another evidence was observed when these same lookout men saw that as soon as the watching tugs caught a glimpse of Shafter's armada they scurried away with the news toward Santiago. Next the Detroit caught the infection of impatience, and when the fleet was abreast of Guantanamo she put on full steam and raced with the tugs for first place in carrying the news.

As the great sea procession moved slowly into view of the blockading fleet the waiting sailors burst into a mighty cheer, and as the line of massive gray hulks was seen by the fighting men on board the transports they sent back the cheer. And so it went on in a majestic and inspiring antiphonal of hurrahs that must have crossed the hills and reached Santiago itself. The flagship fired a salute and sent the Admiral's launch to welcome Shafter, while with signals flying the great transport fleet wheeled into position with every ship's bows facing Santiago.

For the sailors it meant that something was to be done beside swinging up and down in the oily waters of the Caribbean Sea or firing shells at ever demolished and ever repaired earthworks;

Copyright by Mail and Express.   The first landing place of the American

in Cuba—View of Daiquiri.

while to the soldiers it meant something more than the dreary routine of camp life, the vexation of contradictory orders and the cramped life of the transports. For both, it meant action and war at last.

Early next morning, that is, on Tuesday, June 21, Shafter and Sampson went ashore at the little landing-place of Aceraderos to meet Garcia and discuss the best location for landing the troops. Garcia was in favor of landing there and advancing on Santiago from the west, and Sampson was inclined to agree with him, but Shafter, who had closely inspected the coast from a launch the day before, and who had studied the best available maps, decided in favor of Daiquiri, fifteen miles to the east of the Santiago harbor. The General's two chief reasons for this selection were that from Daiquiri could be gained the command of a great plateau directly overlooking Santiago and that the cove contained a railroad wharf. Deference was naturally paid to the wish of the general in command, and the conference broke up after settling the plans of co-operation on the part of the fleet and insurgents.

Daiquiri deserves a paragraph to itself. At it the coast range of Santiago Province, known as the Sierra Cobre, ends in a great peak or massive pile of rocks called La Gran Piedra, which

seems to rise abruptly from the sea. It does
not, however, drop sheer into the sea, but puts
out a number of rugged spurs which have been
cleft in some cataclysm into a series of sharply
cut rocky formations separated by well-defined
chasms or gullies. To some poetic-souled Spaniard, these massive, steep-sided rock masses con-
veyed the impression of altars, and so the locality
is set down on some maps as Las Altares. Between
the beach and the mountain peak stretches a
terrace some fifty feet above the water, and on
this terrace had been built a little settlement of
some twenty frame houses, owned by the Spanish American Iron Company, largely controlled
by the Carnegie Corporation at Pittsburg. The
company had been formed to exploit the iron
mines which lie ten miles away in the mountains
overlooking Santiago harbor. Between the mines
and the landing-place the company had also built
a railroad which at Daiquiri ended in a trestle
bridge and loading chutes, a wharf, a machine
shop, and roundhouse. The surf thunders cease-
lessly in on all the coast except in one little cove
to the west of the railroad wharf, and through this
break and at this wharf and along the sparse
stretches of coral beach it was that the landing
took place on the morning of Wednesday, **June
22.**

The Fall of Santiago.

Before the landing, however, the blockading fleet had its part to play. That part was a dual one. First to insure as nearly as possible a safe landing for the troops, and secondly to confuse the Spaniards as to the selected place of landing. To carry out the second part of this programme the Cubans counterfeited a scene of great preparation at Aceraderos and decoy transports sailed into Cabanas Bay, a small inlet about two miles distant from the entrance. For the first part of the programme Sampson treated the men on the transports to a sight which they will never forget. It was that of twenty miles of bombardment. East and west of Santiago harbor the great fleet of warships stretched along the shore, hurling shells at Aguadores, Cabanas, Siboney, Juragua, Daiquiri, and wherever a roundhouse was noticed, an earthwork seen, or a blockhouse flag distinguished.

The feature of this twenty miles of bombardment was the long distance duel between the Texas and the Socapa battery. It was remarkable for two things. First, as an engagement between a single battleship and a shore battery in which the ship shelled the fort to a standstill, and secondly, as furnishing the unusual example of a Spanish cannoneer hitting his mark and killing his man. The engagement grew out of the feint which had been planned for Cabanas Bay.

Ten transports had been ordered to make a pretense of landing troops there, and the Texas, Scorpion and Vixen had been ordered to shell the blockhouse and surrounding hills as if covering the landing. During the night of June 21-22, the Texas steamed into the shadow of the Cabanas mountains, and daylight found her there waiting for the transports. At seven o'clock four of these appeared and the Texas, to get the shore range, fired a half-dozen rifle shots. They were immediately answered by a gun from high-perched Socapa—a shell in splendid line whistling over the mastheads as the puff of white smoke rose above the fort. The range was found to be five thousand yards and the accuracy of the Spanish gunner at that long distance was such a thorough surprise that Captain Philip decided to give the feint a larger proportion of actuality than had been intended.

The port twelve-inch turret gun was trained on Socapa, and as its report shook the ship a cloud of red dust was seen to rise over the Spanish guns. Forging slowly but steadily nearer, the Texas followed this first shot with a continued and well-aimed fire from the big guns of her port battery. Hit after hit was counted, but unfortunately the Texas had no explosive shells for her turret guns and could only use the solid, armor-piercing shot. It was the crushing force of the impact, therefore, and not the rending of an explosion on which the Texas gunners had to rely for the damage done and which, of course, materially limited the area of possible injury. Each shot was reported to Captain Philip, and aiming instructions given from the bridge. The Spanish reply was fierce and the most accurate that had been experienced. Shells from the Socapa guns moaned over the ship's deck, splashed the water about her, rattled exploding fragments all over her sides and at last struck her fairly. The Indiana, Oregon, Massachusetts, Iowa, and Brooklyn were all lying a few miles away from the encounter, but none thought it worth while taking a hand in the duel, holding that the Texas was able to take care of herself. And so it proved, the battery being fought to a standstill by the Texas and her solid shot in an hour and a half.

The Spaniard's shell was not only noteworthy as killing the first man on an American vessel during the Santiago campaign, but as furnishing a valuable example of the apalling force and destructive qualities of a modern projectile. The shell that struck the Texas was six inches in diameter, was of steel and weighed about seventy-five pounds. It struck the ship's side on the port bow about five feet below the main deck and burst in the forward compartment where there were six 6-pounder guns, three on either side. The crews of all these guns were at quarters, although they had not been in action, and the miracle is that instead of only one man killed and eight wounded, the entire fifteen were not blown into fragments.

At the point of impact the ship's side consisted of steel plates one and a quarter inches thick, the shell piercing it like so much paper; or rather, like so much parchment, the tough metal being folded back in long strips. So trifling had been the resistance of the steel that the shell slipped through it without exploding, and would in all probability have passed out on the other side unexploded had it not struck a metal stanchion amidships. The stanchion was shivered for about two feet of its length, the shell burst, and, while many fragments flew from the explosion as a common center, the larger mass of the broken shell flew forward against the starboard side and bulged out the stout steel plates until they stood as a ridge on the ship's side three inches high.

Where this bulge occurred and on the inside

Copyright by Mail and Express. Debarkation of Shafter

rmy of Invasion at Daiquiri.

of the ship one of the big doubleheaded angle irons of the ship's frame was situated. It was of steel, nearly twice as thick and heavy as a railroad rail, yet two feet of it were scooped out and carried away as though chipped off by a cold chisel. The base of the shell took a downward direction after cutting through the stanchion, plowed a great furrow through the steel deck, hit and broke a steel rib of the ship, broke itself and buried its pieces down through four feet of hemp hawser wound around a cable reel which stood close to the starboard side and shivered the two-foot prism of solid oak on which the hawser was wound. By the explosion of the shell and the fractures made by coming into contact with the stanchion and ribs the shell was resolved into a flying hail of steel splinters which swept along the starboard side for nearly thirty feet, cutting off bolt heads, breaking gun-fittings and actually planing off the paint from the ship's side as cleanly as though it had been laboriously done by hand. The fragmentary result of the explosion was very remarkable. The pieces of steel which were rained everywhere through the compartment weighed about an ounce each, the only fragment of any size being rather less than half of the base of the shell and it was from that fragment that the size of the projectile was learned.

The man who was killed was directly in the path of the shell at the moment of its explosion, and he was literally blown to pieces, although, strangely enough, the comrade to whom he was talking, and who stood at less than an arm's length away, escaped unhurt, except for being knocked down by the force of the explosion. Every other man within radius of the flying fragments was wounded; and not only wounded, but wounded, so to speak, profusely. One gunner was hit with no fewer than fifteen pieces of steel, each about the size of a hazelnut, while other men thirty feet away from the line of shot were found to have a dozen pieces or more of shell in their bodies.

Lastly, as an example of the destructive force of the exploding shell, it may be stated that, when it burst, the gunpowder smoke was forced by the concussion down the ammunition hoists, and into the forward compartments of the ship in such volumes that for a few minutes the crew below were almost suffocated.

This, it is repeated, was the first time that our men had had the opportunity to observe the havoc caused by a modern steel shell filled with high explosives, and as Captain Philip looked at the wrecked compartment and the dead and wounded he was heard to say:

"Well, if a six-inch shell did all that, what would a thirteen-incher do?"

Ever since the arrival of the blockading fleet outside Santiago, General Linares, in command of the Spanish military forces of Santiago Province, had prepared for what he knew must come. Every possible landing-place had been fortified, and naturally in this series of defenses Daiquiri had not escaped attention. Indeed, Daiquiri had been especially looked after, up to a certain point. When our troops landed there they found what was really a magnificent system of defense, earthworks, trenches, pits, breastworks, everything indeed, except the one essential—that of artillery. When the bombardment began there were five hundred Spaniards in charge of these intrenchments, but when the Helena, Hornet and Bancroft tore great gashes in the scrub and brush of the hillsides with their shells; dropped a few 6-inch explosives among the earthworks; filled up the rifle pits with fountains of gravel and dust and even demolished the blockhouse on top of the La Gran Piedra, the garrison concluded that any attempt to keep out the American army of invasion would be somewhat futile.

Steaming down in full view of this theatric act of war the transports formed outside Daiquiri, while the signal went upon the Saguaranca,

"Everybody get ashore." Instantly the flotilla of whaleboats, gigs, barges, and launches which had hung around the transports got into motion. The troopers rushed down the gangway, clambered over the side ladders, pushed their way into the boats, a laughing, cheering, jostling crowd, and loaded the boat to the gunwales in their eagerness to get ashore. As the first boat, in tow of the steam launches, started from the fleet a few Spaniards who had taken refuge behind the blockhouse, ran out and began firing at the loaded boats. As they did so a thousand Cubans who had been brought down during the night from Aceraderos under charge of General Castillo, burst from the woods as if by magic and began firing on the Spaniards. These broke and ran for cover into the western woods, while the New Orleans and Detroit steamed along shore and hastened their departure with a few shells.

All day long the landing went on. Quietly cruising here and there like great sentries on patrol were the vessels of war; in uneven ranks the transports rolled in the short running waves; and between these and the shore there was a constant procession of laden-going and empty-returning boats and puffing launches. All around on the shore side of the view stretched the open crescent of hills, wooded from verge to summit.

On the closer hills could be seen the long shaggy leaves of the palms, the towering cocoanut trees lifting their fronded heads above the lower woods; as a background, a purple peak four thousand feet high; as a foreground, beetling cliffs and wooded glades; and as sounds, the cheery cry of American voices, the unending call of the chafing sea and the wild vivas of Castillo's men as they trooped down to the landing-place to welcome the first of the armies of liberation after having disposed of the Spaniards in the woods.

There had been delay, disappointment and drag in the collection and shipping of Shafter's army, there was none in its debarkation. When night came about twenty small boats had been smashed at the landing-wharf by the surf, two colored troopers of the Tenth Cavalry had been drowned from an overturned boat, a few horses and mules had been drowned while trying to swim ashore, but otherwise ten thousand troops had landed on an enemy's country without mishap and with a celerity and order that will always stand as a precedent in the science of campaigning.

Next day, in order to further expedite the landing, those transports having artillery and the balance of supplies were sent to Siboney

Cove, five miles westward. Wednesday night saw the camp fires sparkling all over the valley and beach around Daiquiri; and Thursday night found the men who had lit these camp fires a long line of marching men with its advance making for Santiago, and other camp fires sparkling all over the valley and beach around picturesque, but ill-starred Siboney.

Where Shafter's army set up its first camp after landing at Daiquiri.

CHAPTER V.

HOW THE ROUGH RIDERS FOUGHT AT LA GUASIMA.

BROADLY speaking, Shafter's plan of campaign was to push his men forward as rapidly as possible after landing, to drive the enemy back toward Santiago, and not to stop in his march on to Santiago until he occupied the plateau and heights which immediately looked down on and commanded the city. He knew from the Cuban scouts that between that point of vantage and Daiquiri the Spanish lay in strength; and he knew from what he had seen from shipboard and the inspection of maps that between Santiago and Daiquiri lay fifteen miles of the roughest country and dense tropical jungle. Roads, however, that were down on the map in large inviting lines turned out, on actual inspection, to be but bridle paths which became mud streams after each downpour, while the transportation of artillery to the front would mean a gigantic task for the engineers whose complete fulfillment would take a far longer time than he in his impatience was willing to consider. But some semblance of work on the roads was an actual necessity, and in order to cover this preparatory work and to clear the territory immediately surrounding the landing, General Shafter deemed it essential to occupy Siboney, a village occupying a commanding position eleven miles up the coast from Daiquiri and eight across country from Santiago.

Not waiting, therefore, for the cavalry horses, siege artillery and balance of the troops, Shafter, in pursuance of his impetuous plans, sent forward General Joseph Wheeler with nine hundred and sixty-four men from his cavalry division, made up of eight troops of Colonel Wood's regiment (the Rough Riders), numbering five hundred; four troops of the First Regular Cavalry, numbering two hundred and forty-four men; and four troops of the Tenth Cavalry (colored), numbering two hundred and twenty, all dismounted. The Rough Riders had pleaded for advance duty and Shafter obliged them.

These Rough Riders furnished the picturesque element of the army. At the very outbreak of hostilities, and indeed before the actual declaration of war, there were vague rumors in the newspapers of the contemplated formation of a cavalry regiment for the Cuban campaign that should be something conjointly approaching a

The Fall of Santiago.

Buffalo Bill show, a round-up of Western cowboys and a congregation of cross-country huntsmen. The credit for the initiative of the idea lies in amiable dispute between General Miles and Theodore Roosevelt, but from the very first the name of Roosevelt was more intimately associated in the public mind with the idea than that of any one else.

When war broke out he was Assistant Secretary of the Navy, but immediately following on McKinley's proclamation he resigned and was by the president named as Lieutenant-Colonel of the First United States Volunteer Cavalry, of which Captain Leonard Wood, assistant surgeon in the regular army, was appointed Colonel. The work of organization was immediately begun by Colonel Wood and aides, who chose the Western States as the best recruiting ground from which to select their men. Dr. Wood, as he was generally known, was admirably adapted for this recruiting work, having had a long experience in Western army life. Truth to tell, there was little need of recruiting, for with the first intimation that the regiment was to be an accomplished fact, the War Department was swamped with appeals for information as to points at which enlistments might be made.

Every man in the country who could ride a

horse, or who had an inclination to do so, appeared to imagine that he was the man of all men who should be a trooper. Colonel Wood was, however, determined that his regiment should only contain the very best of horsemen and fighting material. The line was drawn rigorously at toughs and incapables. Every man was a picked man and when the regiment was finally declared to be completed at San Antonio, Texas, it proved to be an aggregation of extremes, record and experience that was unique in military history. The members ranged from cotillion leader to bronco buster, from society roysterer to policeman, from dead-shot cowboy to champion golfer, from a record-making college runner to a steer brander of Skull Valley, from a champion football player of the East to a bear hunter of the West. Dancers, polo players, good fellows, old soldiers, bad men, firemen—the wildest congregation of dudes and daredevils surely that was ever brought together. A few of the names and a word of those who bore them should find a place here.

"Dead Shot Jim" Simpson, from Albuquerque, N. M., could put a rifle ball through a jack rabbit's eyes while riding a wild horse a thousand yards off. Woodbury Kane, a cousin of John Jacob Astor, was equally at home as a polo player and a yachtsman. "Lariat Ned" Perkins, from Trinidad, Col., had the reputation of being able to make his twisted rope as deadly as a rifle. Willie Tiffany, of New York, was a cousin of the Belmonts, the nephew of Commodore Perry and an authority on fine raiment. "Rocky Mountain Bill" Jenkins was a mighty hunter of the grizzly and was, literally, always loaded for bear. Hamilton Fish, Jr., of New York, was the descendant of a long line of famous men and had established a reputation in which energy and animal spirits were only equaled by good fellowship and lovable disposition. "Bronco George" Brown, of Arizona, had killed his five men, but they all went down for cattle stealing, for cheating at cards, or for impudence to women. Reggie Reynolds, son of Mrs. Lorillard B. Reynolds, was quarterback on a Yale team and a handshaking acquaintance of the Prince of Wales. "Fighting Bob" Wilson, of Wyoming, was the terror of the rustlers on his range. I. Townsend Burden, Jr., was the son of a great millionaire of New York City, and proud of his record on the football field.

And so, with much dust and jingle of spurs, the plainsmen and mountaineers of the West came trooping into San Antonio; with valets, bathtubs, and dress-suit cases, the dudes and brokers of the East rolled into town in parlor cars; with the outfits of the fop, the handbag of the hardy experienced man, and with no kits at all, save the things on his back and the beast he bestrode, the Rough Riders gathered together.

But when once together every division of class and belonging was swept away. There was comradeship from the start, for each man was a United States trooper, sworn to serve his country and to fight for it at thirteen dollars a month with rations and uniform. The uniform, by the bye, was as picturesque as the men. Made of gray grass cloth, cool and light of texture, with pipings and facings of blue, with a sombrero turned up and fastened at the side with a rosette, armed with a Krag-Jorgensen carbine, two revolvers and a machete, the Rough Riders presented a decidedly dashing and warlike appearance. In their camp life they settled down to hard work with an energy, obedience and good will that were glorious. Much of this hard work was given to the breaking and drilling of the horses, yet by one of the ironical strokes of fate the first time the Rough Riders went into battle they went afoot.

Such were the Rough Riders, who with the First Regulars, a regiment noted in every army post for its steady valor, and the Tenth troopers,

with their Western reputation as always wanting
to fight and always fighting as devils when that
want was gratified, at daybreak of June 23,
marched out of Daiquiri on the road to Siboney,
accompanied by a body of Cuban scouts. The
first halt was made at the little village of Dema-
jayabo, and for these and all other names to be
mentioned reference had better be had to the
accompanying map.

That march was a trial to the souls and condition of the men. They had heard of the Cuban
forests and the Cuban heat, but the most vivid
imagination had pictured nothing approaching
the reality. The road was a mule path and not
always an ordinarily good mule path at that.
Where it did not pass through swamps of malo-
dorous mud it was a winding lane of irony-red
earth, which rose in clouds of dust as the men
tramped on, filled their eyes and noses, was plas-
tered on their streaming faces, and found its way
even between the flaps of the buttoned gaiters.
On each side of the path rose the thick steamy
jungle, so profuse in its vegetation that its entangling vines and piercing thorns stretched
across it almost at every step. Sometimes there
were breaks in the chaparral, but on these open
spaces the sun beat down with uninterrupted
fervor, so that it was not a relief but rather a

choice of evils between the blazing experience of the bare spots and the boiling experience of the woods. As was the case at the fight over the hills at Guantanamo, the men started in heavy accoutrements, in full marching order, but as the day grew and the heat with it, the men threw away not only their blanket rolls and provision haversacks but even their clothing, until the path side looked as though it had been traversed rather by an army in retreat than by one in advance.

Juragua was reached at night without the faintest opposition from the Spaniards, the Cuban scouts bringing in information that the enemy which had been in some force at Siboney had fallen back on the Sevilla road and had halted and intrenched themselves at a small settlement named La Guasima, some three or four miles beyond Siboney. Many of the men had fallen from exhaustion, and the detachment of Rough Riders, which had been in charge of the dynamite gun, with which it was expected to do great things, had insisted on bringing this weapon with them, so that it was long after dusk when the last stragglers were brought in by the rearguard. General Castillo, who was in command of the Cuban scouts, made out a rough map of La Guasima for General Wheeler and it was de-

cided to continue the march beyond Siboney at daybreak of the 24th and attack the Spanish position.

There were two roads leading to La Guasima, and it was decided to divide the American forces so as to attack the Spaniards from two quarters. Colonel Wood's regiment was sent to approach the enemy on the left hand or mountain road, while Wheeler and Young, with the First and Tenth, and three Hotchkiss mountain guns, were to attack the enemy on the main or valley road. Young's command had somewhat the shorter road and they started by throwing out a strong scouting line in order to give Wood's men a chance to work round to the left. The troopers, as they lay at Juragua, had heard the Spaniards felling the trees before daybreak and judged that they were throwing up barricades, but on account of the echoing hills could not exactly locate the spot from which the sounds came. With the general locality of the Spaniards and the character of their position and their strength General Wheeler was, however, measurably well informed, as his plan of battle indicates.

In the first confused reports of what follows the belief was entertained that the Rough Riders had fallen into an ambuscade, but except insomuch as nearly all the Spanish fighting was done from the ambush of protecting timber, dense screens of foliage and well-hidden rifle pits, the fight at La Guasima scarcely possessed any greater share of an attack from ambush than did the battles of San Juan and El Caney. No clearer refutation of the ambush story is needed than the fact that on the night before the battle General Young sent for Colonel Wood and said to him:

"Colonel, Castillo's scouts tell me that the Spaniards have taken a very strong position near the junction of the trail over the mountain to Sevilla and the valley road. It is evidently their belief that they can stop or drive us back if we try to advance, but I think the brigade can fight and win the first battle of the war to-morrow morning."

Althought last to start, the First and Tenth Cavalry men were the first to open the action. The road over which they went cheerily along was moderately good, and the men being used to hot weather marching made good progress. When they rose from the valley on to one of the foothills which rose in chaotic prodigality all about they discovered the enemy, hurried a Hotchkiss gun to the crest and began blazing away.

Right across a narrow valley which lay in front

of them rose another hill, and on it they plainly distinguished the Spanish position. The main body of the Spaniards was posted around two blockhouses near the summit, flanked by irregular intrenchments of stone and trees. These intrenchments were in the shape of a broad V or horseshoe, the point of which was toward the trail and road where they came together at the foot of the hill. In this position they were enabled to offer a triple fire against any advancing force. Between the intrenchments and the trails was a dense thicket, and as it proved afterward, this thicket was alive with sharpshooters and guerrillas. The main body of the regulars was streaming up the valley road after the advance men with their Hotchkiss, but the Rough Riders could not be seen owing to the broken nature of the country and its densely wooded character. As a matter of fact, they were, at that time, pushing along the trail which led over the crest of a hill much similar in elevation and character to that occupied by the regulars. If this description is at all clear it will be seen, therefore, that in the confusion of hills there were three that were distinct points of interest. To the right that occupied by the Regulars, to the left that over which the Rough Riders were climbing and, between these two flanking elevations, the central hill on which the Spaniards were posted.

The distance between the two hills occupied by our men was about half a mile. The Hotchkiss pieces began the fight at seven-thirty, and in reply to the first rattling sweep of the machine guns the whole front of the hill facing them burst into volleys from the Spanish Mausers. The troopers were instantly ordered to lie down in the road along which they were strung, General Young's command being "Don't shoot until you see something to shoot at," which he yelled to his men as stripped to the waist they crawled and squirmed into some position from which they could get a chance to see their enemies. Almost immediately thereafter came the crack of the Krag-Jorgensens from Colonel Wood's men and the engagement was on.

Meanwhile, the Rough Riders had pushed their way over the cactus-lined mountain trail. They had marched two miles when they came across the body of a dead Cuban and this evidence of the Spanish whereabouts was sufficient to admonish the men that an especially sharp lookout was necessary. The dead scout was found by the skirmishers of Troop L, which was under command of Captain Allyn K. Capron. He immediately deployed his men and sent back word to

The Fall of Santiago. 107

Colonel Wood of his discovery. The regiment was hurried up, but before it could be well deployed the whole line of thickets to their front and right broke out with the sharp, sibillant sing of the Spanish rifles. As at Guantanamo the Spaniards fired in such rapid volleys by holding the rifle at the hip and pumping the shots out with the quick fanning of the right hand on the lever bar that the discharges actually sounded as though they were from machine guns.

Word was passed along the American line to fire right and left and in front, and for an hour and a half this fight of gunnery continued. Owing to the facts that the Spanish were so completely under cover and that they used smokeless powder it was almost impossible to direct any answering fire that might be effective, but by careful watching a Spanish head was seen here or there or some sharpshooter was seen slipping from cover to cover, and wherever either head or sharpshooter was seen an American bullet was sure to find its mark.

In the first blaze of the Mausers' Hamilton Fish was killed. He was in the advance as the head of the skirmishers turned the crest of the hill and though the order to take cover was immediate, the commanding position of the Spanish riflemen was such that they could send a dropping fire into the men as they lay down. Alongside Fish lay Ed Culver, a Cherokee Indian, and the same long Mauser bullet that struck the brave roystering aristocrat struck the half-breed, for it passed through Fish's body and lodged in that of Culver. When Fish was struck he said to Culver: "I am wounded," to which Culver made reply: "And I am killed." But it was not so, for it was Fish who died when they took him back and set him under a tree with his face to the enemy, while the half-breed Indian lived and, though shot through the lung, continued to empty his rifle at the Spaniards until his ammunition pouch was exhausted and the gun fell from his hands.

Soon after this Captain Capron was shot as he walked along the line cheering his men. He had taken a rifle from a wounded man and was firing when the bullet struck him. As the troopers lifted him to carry him to the rear he shook his head and said: "No, place me here. I want to see this thing out."

And so he did, for they propped up his head so that the firing line was visible, and when the captain died the troopers were chasing down the valley and up the hill and the day was practically won.

When it was seen that only a desperate charge

would win the day, orders were sent along the line for an advance and then began the first of those cyclonic rushes which later won Santiago, and which so amazed the Spaniards. By all the rules of warfare to which they were accustomed, the Spanish soldiers held an impregnable position, while the fire to which the Americans were exposed was one that could only force a retreat. But the Americans had quite another idea and when the word came to advance they leaped from cover with yell that rang from end to end of the line, and went sweeping down the sides of their hills, across the valleys beneath, and up the central mountain.

As at Guantanamo the long line of men would rush forward, loading as they rushed, then halt with a rock-like poise, aim and fire, and then rush on again. On the right could be heard the screaming negroes of the Tenth, in the center the First Cavalry moved forward like a living wall, while to the left the Rough Riders, yelling like Indians, pressed forward, Roosevelt in the lead with a Krag-Jorgensen in his hands and yelling as loud as the wildest man from the West.

The Spanish fire was steady enough for a time, but nothing could stand the charges of our men. So fast was the pace of the soldiers across the valley and up the hill that they threw away their side arms and accouterments in order to move the faster. The Spaniards moved back as the men advanced, but made a stand in the intrenchments and blockhouse. Between these and the line of advance there was an open space of rolling land, some three hundred yards across. It was when the Americans emerged from the bush into this open space that the Spanish made their last attempt to drive back the attacking line, and it was when they saw how the dismounted cavalrymen swept across the clearing notwithstanding the way in which they went down under the close range Mauser fire that they gave up the impossibility of resisting men who did not know when they were beaten, broke and ran. On swept our men, and with a mighty cheer the hill was won, Rough Riders and Regulars, white and black, shaking hands and cheering again when they found breath—brothers in arms indeed.

Inside the trenches were many Spanish dead; within the blockhouse were seventeen more, and a long line of wagons with wounded could be seen making its way down the Santiago trail. Altogether and from after reports the estimate is made that the Spanish losses at La Guasima numbered fully one hundred and fifty. Our losses were, of the First United States Volunteer Cavalry, eight killed, thirty-four wounded; of

The Fall of Santiago.

the First United States Cavalry, seven killed, eight wounded; of the Tenth United States Cavalry, one killed, ten wounded; that is, out of a total strength of nine hundred and sixty-four men, sixteen were killed and fifty-two wounded.

Beside these losses to the combatants, Edward Marshall, a New York Journal correspondent, was seriously and for a time it was believed fatally wounded. He was in the advance with the Rough Riders as they moved up the trail and was plodding, struggling along with the best of them when the murderous volley from the Spaniards stopped the advance. Though warned of his danger he had taken a place underneath a royal palm from which he could note the progress of the fight, when a Mauser bullet passed from the groin, the point of entrance, through the body and shattered the base of the spine. Though told by the surgeons on the field that the blow was a mortal one, Marshall kept his ground. It was an illustration of another kind of bravery than that of the fighting men. It was the bravery of duty.

CHAPTER VI.

HOW THE ARMY MARCHED TO THE FRONT.

THE skirmish of La Guasima took place on June 24; the first assault on the outposts of Santiago occurred on July 1. Between those dates, however, much was done, and while that much did not include any more brushes with the Spaniards, it was a time of hard and testing experience. The story of the great fighting will be found in the next chapters, but he who would read these chapters with understanding had better read this.

Anticipatory descriptions, it is true, are always more or less looked upon as halts in a fair-running story, but sometimes these halts are necessary for the full appreciation of the development of that story. The description of the battles of San Juan and El Caney, however lamely told, cannot fail to make the pulses beat, but unless one puts oneself more nearly into the place of the American soldier than would be the case should the story jump from the landing at

Daiquiri to the dash up the great hills that form the outposts of the Gran Mesa, one will not get truly into the very heart of the task which was set the American soldier to do.

When the news of the landing at Daiquiri reached Washington the great war maps of Santiago were spread out, and it was noticed with satisfaction that from the landing-place there ran a broad highway over the hills to Santiago. But as was the case when studying the road that was taken by the Rough Riders, the inaccuracies of the great map of Cuba, compiled though it was by the Spanish government, were astonishing. For instance, the railroad, which really ends at Daiquiri, is set down as turning inland from a point some five or six miles to the east of its actual terminus. The suburb of El Caney is written Guay, and is located five miles to the west of where it really is; Siboney is not on the maps at all, while towns which are marked inland were found to be on the seacoast, and those which were set down on the cliffs were found to be miles back in the woods. To add to these contradictions of topography it was found that the residential nomenclature was not at all that of the map-maker, while the Cubans, possibly as another evidence of their love of freedom, had from two to half a dozen different names for the same place.

But, perplexing as these contradictions and mislocations were, they faded into insignificance before the upset of transportation plans and the new set of physical problems which were caused and presented by the vast difference of what was seen on the maps and what was found on land. In the matter of roads it may be set down at once that the invading army found none that could be called military highways. What it did find were trails and bridle paths. On the maps and from the sea were shown and could be seen the larger outlines of the Sierra Cobre, but these broad outlines concealed a mass of smaller, but steep, declivities, cross-running hills, swampy gullies and rocky spurs that lined the face of nature as thickly as do the wrinkles on that of an old Breton fisherwoman.

The Gran Mesa was to Major-General Shafter the great alluring spot from the very outset. To gain that plateau was the central point of his strategy. That plateau was, as it were, like the palm of an inviting hand laid down midway on the map between Daiquiri and Santiago. To the west of the plateau, that is Santiagowards, it was flanked by a system of hills whose slopes trended down to the city. The occupation of

this plateau therefore, with its bulwark of hills, meant the command, the actual investment, of Santiago. To throw his men right across the country, until it should form a line across these uplands, was therefore Shafter's first necessity. It was, to use the same figure of speech, as though, having gained a place on that inviting palm of the Gran Mesa, the hand were turned until it rested on edge, forming a living line of circumvallation which was to move closer and closer on the invested city.

Two other factors were to be considered in the coming fight: First the possible reinforcement of General Linares by General Pando; second, the possible escape of General Linares from Santiago when he found that the day had gone against him. Shafter had fourteen thousand seven hundred men; the best, the most reliable, estimates placed the army of Linares at eleven thousand four hundred and thirty, while Pando was reported as having nine thousand under him at Holquin. To prevent Linares from slipping away from and Pando from slipping into Santiago, therefore, it was an essential that—still keeping to the simile of the hand—the finger tips should be crooked until the living line which it indicated had closed around Santiago Bay on the north and westward. So the moving and crushing process was to go on until Santiago was in the American grasp.

By looking at the accompanying map it will be seen that were a line drawn across the three points, Aguadores, San Juan and El Caney and then curved around to the westward, it would roughly form a parallel line to that of the Santiago Bay shore. These three places, because of their position and because they were the foci of the Spanish defenses, were therefore selected as the three main points in the plan of occupation and investment, with San Juan as the center, El Caney as the right and Aguadores as the left of attack. General Lawton's division was to assault El Caney; General Duffield was to march against Aguadores, and Generals Wheeler and Kent were to advance against San Juan.

This broad outline of Shafter's plan of attack is all that need be given here. What is next to be shown is what our men encountered as they moved into position to carry out this plan of attack. In order that there might be as little congestion as possible and in pursuance with the commanding officer's policy of hurry work, the troops were hastened forward from the landing-places as rapidly as possible. The next days saw the entire debarkation of the first army of invasion, this work having been expedited by sending some of the transports into the adjoining cove of Siboney after it had been ridden of the enemy by the dismounted cavalry on June 24. It was a fatal expediteness as it proved, for though the selection of this enticing, vine-embowered little hamlet by the sea was undeniably useful as a second and additional point from which to hurry troops inland and new base of supplies, it proved afterward to be the starting point of a plague that meant a shallow Cuban grave for many a good man.

In the first days the march toward Santiago was generally begun in the early morning or the late afternoon, but toward the last, regiments, companies and troops were sent forward at any hour, no matter what the position of the sun. Each regiment, company or troop went forward with a swing, but as the days of weary climbing through brush and undergrowth, over rocks and across gullies went on, the very life seemed to go out of the men.

The curious tourists who will flock to Santiago and walk back over the road from the lovely suburb of El Caney to Daiquiri and note that between the metropolis of eastern Cuba and the landing-place of the iron company there is a road, and a moderately good one, will fail to understand the true character of the Via Dolorosa

over which our troops had to make their way.
Before these troops had stamped it into something like a roadbed and the engineers had been fitfully at work, before the brush had been cut away and the swamps logged into something approaching passability, every step was a labor. Then the roads outside the one main route were simply errant paths through dense tropical forests, over sun-scorched patches of desert and through rank grass and tangled weeds which were as ropes and nets to the feet of the men. There were no bridges over the streams, no trestles across the gullies, and nowhere were the paths wide enough for two vehicles. What this moment was the trickling remnant of a stream in a rocky bed became a torrential river after five minutes' of cloudburst in the mountains; the engineers' makeshift bridges were swept away time and again; wagon trains were stalled all along the line of march, communication was at times entirely interrupted between the front and the shore depots, and as an example of the condition of things it may be stated that during the four days preceding the surrender it was only possible to get to the front one light battery of the six brought by General Randolph, while not a single one of the heavy siege guns was taken off the transports at Siboney.

The Fall of Santiago.   119

The experience which had been that of the First and Tenth Cavalry and Rough Riders was repeated in the case of the troops in the main advance. When they started on the march every man went in full marching order. That meant rifle, cartridges, bayonet, pistol, canteen, poncho, half of a shelter tent, rations and whatever else the man might like to burden himself with. The men had worn these traps on the hot but breezy days when they were in Camp Black, on the hotter and breezeless days when they were at Chickamauga, in the sweltering pine groves back of Tampa, and in the oven-like plains of our great middle basin, but none of these experiences had fitted them for what they were enduring now. As the regiments moved from the beaches up into the trails, they were as presentable and trim a set of fighting men as one would wish to see. When they had got into position along the line of attack they were as untrim, un-uniformed and bedraggled a lot of fighting men as ever did great deeds. As they struggled up the hillsides and tramped down the slopes the packs shifted and slipped and bore down on them; and as the sun beat down on the lines of men that were stretched for miles through this terrible country the packs and bundles and impedimenta slid about as though they were alive, and gained in weight from pounds to tons. In the woods the packs caught in the overhanging underbrush and sent the men stumbling and falling. In the open places the sun was like a furnace and the packs were like lead. At last one man threw his blanket away and then was begun over and carried out that scene of derobement and dispossession which had marked the progress of the dismounted cavalrymen. Blankets were strung along the bushes as though some flock of gigantic sheep had gone through and had left tufts of wool on every bush. After the blankets went cans of meat, then the shelter tents, then the cooking outfit, then coats and underclothes and anything else except his fatigue uniform, his rifle and cartridges, for these last two essentials every man kept.

This was while the sun was blazing, but when the sun set there came another evil out of this strange land. The awful heat passed and with the night air came a penetrating, damp chill that seemed to touch the bone.

All during the day not even the liveliest imagination could conceive of such heat being followed by any such poetic relief as "the cool of the evening," nor were the evenings cool, but it was at that crisis of the night, the early hours of dawn, that the searching, penetrating cold came upon the men. So cold indeed was it at this time, partly by comparison with the hot day and partly as a positive condition, that the men were actually awakened shivering at about two or three o'clock. The first consideration then was warmth and dryness, but when another hour or so had passed and reveille had sounded at four o'clock another change had come and exercise seemed the desideratum in the fresh of the morning. Another hour or two and as the sun mounted and the pitiless heat grew apace all the men wanted to do was to sit and rest. So the changes went on, from cool humidity to hot humidity, each change sapping away the very vitality of the men.

A still more serious result to the men came from their stripping themselves during their march. Not only did they throw away their heavy clothing, but they rejected their food supplies, trusting to luck and the supply trains; or they abandoned their rations for the simple reason that the rations were heavy and they were hot. But the supply trains, as has been intimated, were as rare as Sunday railway trains in Vermont, and the situation of the camps soon became a serious one. Officers and men were alike in their plight, but all through the ranks there was no complaining. The ready helping hand of good companionship was there and the clever combining, lending and aiding that went far toward relieving the individual discomforts, and that welded the companionship of the men into those strong bonds of friendship formed in times of trial which never break and live forever.

One great practical lesson in the economy of the commissariat was learned in this march. When the men left the landing-places they carried cans of preserved food—admirable forms of protected diet under certain conditions, but cans of meat and vegetables are decidedly lumpy and uncomfortable adjuncts to a march through a tropical forest, and, it will be remembered, they were among the first things to be slung into the bush. Between a future meal of bacon and beans and a present bumping battering ram there was no choice, and the banging thing was discarded. The three essentials of food that the men clung to were coffee, hardtack and bacon—the standard rations—and it was proved again that with these three simples an army could be kept in well-sustained and fighting trim.

The men on march, too, furnished a practical solution of the water question. Before the invasion of Cuba there were many learned discussions on water supply, the hygiene of water-drinking, clever arrangements for filtration and the establishment of condensing plants. Scientific men, military men and fadful men wrote and talked about the water of Cuba and the water which our troops were to get while in Cuba. It was to be boiled and filtered and never drunk unless filtered and boiled. In theory, the columns of learned matter which were printed and the hours of clever talk which were given to the subject were admirable. In practice, the men drank the first water they came to. When the Spaniards withdrew from Daiquiri and Siboney they partially destroyed the water systems of those two places, but our engineers repaired them and the water taken from those tanks was freely used without boiling or filtering, and without any ill effects. In the inland march the men crossed many streams, large and small, and the men drank of these streams without boiling or filtering and apparently without any ill effects.

The water that did bother them was that which came down in sheets, cold drenching sheets, every time the black clouds swept across the Sierra Cobre. They had heard of the wet season in Cuba, but as their experience of Cuban heat transcended their imagination of it, so was it the case in their conception and experience of a rainy afternoon near Santiago. Before the storm came, the sultry air grew still sultrier. From the trampled, beaten, crushed, tropical undergrowth rose sickening odors and heavy miasmatic mists. As the heat grew fiercer, the odors and mists grew heavier. Every life-giving quality of the air seemed to be squeezed out of it, and even the myriad insects and crawling reptiles were quieted.

Then, just as the sizzling heat reached a spot where it apparently could go no further and be bearable, a zigzag flash, a thunderclap, and a cataract of ice-cold rain came simultaneously, and every man was soaked and shivering. If the men were marching, they found themselves suddenly wading through swift running streams of cold muddy water, with what they had on changed from its reek of perspiration into cold, wet, clinging garments. If the men were in camp or the trenches, their fires were put out and every ditch became a mud pool. For two or three hours the icy water fell, until all the hillsides were moving with a floating mass of mud and leaves, and the muddy water in the trails had risen from sole to ankle and from ankle to legging top. Then, as suddenly as it had begun, the storm would come to an end, the sun came out hotter than ever; the wet ground steamed; horrible crawling, flying things filled the muggy air, and from shivering the men passed to gasping. Yet through it all the men pressed forward, far less complainingly perhaps, than they would have done had they been at home and a summer shower had spoiled their picnic.

The flying pests of Cuba the men found bad enough, but it was the consensus of opinion that bad as gnats, mosquitoes and beetles were they were far less dreaded than the land crabs, and this because of the repulsiveness of the latter creatures. These hard-shelled, crawling things were everywhere, in the woods and on the plains; crowds of them in the gullies and troops of them on the hilltops. No matter where the men marched or where they halted, there were the squads, regiments and battalions of the land crabs, until the men were sickened at the sight and began to believe that, like sharks following a ship, the land crabs actually followed the army, a species of horrible camp follower. In size the land crabs varied from four to twelve inches across the carapace, its covering area being, of course, increased by legs and claws, the latter qu to formidable implements.

They are rather gay-colored creatures, their tints ranging from light-green to dark-blue, the blue crab being the most objectionable. They are decidedly gregarious and travel in hosts, and are not inclined to let anything interfere with their line of progression. Individually, the crab walks in a decidedly aggressive attitude. The eye stalks are thrust out, the body tilted sidewise, and the claws thrown upward and outward like sabers. He has the strange fashion of moving forward for a few feet then rapidly scuttling either to the right or to the left, and then as abruptly walking backward. As this decidedly eccentric method of advance seems to animate the whole body of crabs, the aggregate result is that this whole body of crabs seems to move along in a wave-like motion. As they move they clash their claws and rattle among themselves, so that when making their way through the brush or grass the sound of their progress is so singularly like that of men marching that our pickets constantly mistook the advance of the crabs for the sudden onslaught of the enemy. As the men marched the crabs marched too in parallel columns; and when the men halted for the night the crabs swarmed over the sleeping men and acted in a generally inquisitive and unpleasant fashion. Many stories were spread by imaginative Cubans of the uncanny results of crab-nips, of nocturnal attacks on protruding toes, and of the desperate results that would follow should a crab desire the protruding toe; of their living in the poisoned shade of witch trees and so on, but in plain truth they are the creeping buzzards of the West Indies, and aid those disagreeable looking bird in the great work of scavengering.

A glance at the map will show that Santiago lies at the head of a landlocked bay, six miles from the sea. Aguadores lies two and a half miles east of the entrance to the harbor and is directly south of Santiago itself, the bay shore curving northward to El Morro. Four miles southeast of Santiago is the ridge of San Juan. Three miles northwest of Santiago is the suburb of El Caney, which is six miles due north of San Juan. A line from El Caney to Aguadores through San Juan would be a fairly straight line in a southwesterly direction. Both San Juan and El Caney are perched upon hills, the flat-topped steep-sided formation before alluded to as the distinguishing mark of Las Altares characterizing the scores of hills into which the country is broken to the east of Santiago Bay. On the flat tops of these hills the rich Santiagoans had built themselves broad-eaved country seats, or farmhouses, the altitude of the locality and the general park-like character of the country making these plantation houses charming homes.

The Spanish engineers were quick to see the

strategical importance of these hills as natural defenses and were most ingenious in their elaborations upon nature's work. The farmhouses, or country seats, were quickly and effectually transformed into forts by filling the spaces between the piazza pillars with ramparts of broken stone or earth bags and by breaking out loopholes in the walls. Where no farmhouses stood they built a blockhouse of planks and stone, and perched these so promiscuously and generously about that from any commanding elevation one might count a score of these tiny forts.

As a further elaboration in the system of defense the engineers made free use of Weyler's great barbed-wire idea. Barbed-wire fences were found bordering the trails and it was learned that these had been erected for the simple purpose of keeping the Cubans in the right path, any Cuban caught straying in the woods being summarily treated as one who had crossed the deathline; or at least as one who was a poacher on preserves, or a suspicious character. Barbed-wire was strung around the approaches to every blockhouse. The Rough Riders had found it impeding their way when they charged the hill at La Guasima and the men who fought at San Juan and El Caney found that, like the experience of Cuban heat and Cuban jungle, the

From photograph by J. C. Hemment. Copyright, 1898, by W. R. Hearst.
The trenches with their barbed wire protections on the San Juan hill. After Kent's men had emptied the ditches of the dead Spaniards, they leaped into the pits and turned their guns on the fleeing enemy.

The Fall of Santiago.

reality went far ahead of even the most vivid anticipation.

The quartermaster-general had been forwarned of the barbed-wire defenses which the American army would meet with in Cuba and had forearmed the men with nippers, but nippers, like cans of corned beef, are hard things to carry on a hot march, and were among the first of the impedimenta to be dropped. Moreover, when the barbed-wire fences were met with they did not yield to the nippers as easily as had been anticipated. The nippers had been supplied on the belief that the barbed-wire abatis was composed simply of wire fences of from four to eight feet high, and that a few vigorous nips along the posts would result in loose strands that could easily be thrown back and so open the way to the men. It was found, however, that the barbed-wire defenses were not built on this simple fence plan. Instead of being stretched in regular strands the wire was strung from tree to tree at the most irregular heights possible. Sometimes, a strand was found fastened to a stump and running thence to a neighboring tree at such an angle as to carry it ten feet from the ground, from which it slanted down to the next tree to a height of three or four feet from the ground. Six or eight strands of the wire would thus be run irregularly along for miles, and it meant a hunt to discover each individual strand.

To have done with the barbed-wire question so as not to let it interfere with the plain description of the fight, it may be said here that both at San Juan and El Caney it was frequently found that the only way to discover the presence of a barbed-wire fence was to run against it. At the last slope-down of a steep hill, in the pools and rivers, strung along through the rank grass and surrounding the rifle pits and trenches in a perfect maze—were these abominable wire fences. Nor were they made of single strands, but were often most elaborately put together, being in some cases twisted together like ropes and so matted that it was impossible to get a finger in between the interstices. Before such unusual and artful use of barbed-wire the nippers with which the American soldiers were provided were not much more useful than cheese scoops would be as rock drills.

To the array of blockhouses and forts and the tangle of barbed-wire, the Spanish engineers had added admirably devised lines of deep but narrow trenches, running in such lines that the riflemen holding them could easily move from one range to another. Line after line of these trenches and rifle pits was found at every pos-

The Fall of Santiago.

sible point of vantage, the whole system of defense exciting the admiration of our engineers.

Thus it was that the army pushed its way into the line of attack, and it was after passing through such trials of advance, climate, country, and pests that it found itself, on the night of June 31, drawn up across the island in a great broken line of three divisions from El Caney in the interior to Aguadores on the sea. But they had all been natural difficulties to overcome and bear, none of battle, for, save for the brush at La Guasima, the Spanish had made no resistance to the army's advance. The men had practically landed without opposition, and just as it was Shafter's bustling policy to push his men forward until they occupied the outposts of Santiago, so it turned out now to be the Spaniard's equally well-settled plan of campaign to let that advance be made until those outposts were reached, and then to defend them to the death.

CHAPTER VII.

HOW EL CANEY WAS CARRIED.

In the future days of criticism much will doubtless be said as to the wisdom, indecision and fortuitous fulfillment of Shafter's plan of campaign. But this book is a record of events and not a discussion of military technicalities.

Doubtless Shafter expected to do much more in certain directions than he did; and in other directions much more was done than he had anticipated would be the case. The capture of El Caney was to be effected, so Shafter thought, in the early hours of the day, after which the troops were to join those before San Juan and the day was to be wound up in a joint attack on and capture of San Juan. As it turned out, El Caney offered a more stubborn resistance than did San Juan, and by the time the troops forming the right of the general advance had carried the suburb, San Juan had been stormed and taken.

It is a fact, too, that Shafter planned the reduction of an intrenched city without seige guns and mortars, these having been left on the Orizaba. But in explanation of this it may be said that Shafter, in the choice between an assault by unsupported infantry and waiting for the engineers to put the road into sufficiently good condition to admit of moving the siege batteries to the front, decided that it was better to attack the Spaniards by his army as it stood with such field pieces as could be easily moved forward, rather than to expose his men to climatic effects. As the men stood they were yet full of the strength and vitality they had brought with them, but subject them to a long exposure to summer rains and heat, argued Shafter, and the debilitating powers of these enemies would seriously diminish the fighting quality of his army.

The disposition of the army, as decided on at a council of war on June 29, was as follows: Lawton's Division, the Second, was sent against El Caney; Kent's Division, the First, and Wheeler's Cavalry Division were to proceed against San Juan; Duffield's Brigade was to move on Aguadores. In the order of description, the fight and fortunes of the men at El Caney will be first taken up. The Second Division was constituted as follows:

First Brigade, General Ludlow commanding,

Eighth, Twenty-second, and Second Massachusetts.

Second Brigade, Colonel Miles commanding Fourth, First, and Twenty-fifth.

Third Brigade, General Chaffee commanding, Twelfth, Seventh, and Seventeenth.

Captain Capron's Battery E, First Artillery, was to shell the town and General Garcia, as our ally, held a thousand Cubans under him. Later in the day General Bates' Independent Brigade was attached to Lawton's division.

General Lawton, following the council of war, not only went over the field carefully on the map, but in company with his three brigade commanders made a reconnaissance on June 30. Lawton reported that he found the Spanish ground much stronger than he had anticipated, and in the absence of heavy artillery he suggested that he move his forces at night and so get into position for delivering his blow in the early morning. Lawton failed to get proper support for his suggestion and, with the exception of Chaffee's Brigade, the division slept on its arms. General Chaffee, however, worked his men well to the northward all during June 30, and before the night was over had his men in position, well intrenched to the north and east of El Caney. At early dawn on July 1 the other

From photograph by J. C. Hemment.   Copyright, 1898, by W. R. Hearst
Fort and block-house at El Caney.   It was across this open swale and up this pyramidical hill that Lawton's men had to advance in order to capture the fort.   The village of El Caney lies behind the hill and below the fort to the left.

troops of Lawton's Division made their way to the positions previously designated for them to occupy. Ludlow's Brigade and Garcia's Cubans moved still further around El Caney until they rested on the west of the village in order to cut off the retreat of the Spaniards when they should be driven out of the town and attempt to retire. Colonel Miles' Brigade took up a position to the east of El Caney; Bates, on his arrival, forming to the southeast.

By this disposition of troops it will be seen the division occupied a broad segment of a circle with El Caney as the center. Dominating El Caney was a stone fort perched on the very apex of a hill, which looked like a minature peak, and at whose base lay the village. The fort was a mediæval affair, four square, except for a round bastion at each corner. But mediæval as it was in construction, it was filled with men armed with modern guns and proved a veritable citadel. It was toward this fort that Captain Capron directed the fire of his light battery of four guns. He had planted his battery before sunrise on a bluff about a mile and a half distant from the town, there being a deep swale of rolling land between the fort and the battery, the emplacement of the battery having been effected without the enemy's discovering the move.

It was yet dark when at five-forty on the morning of July 1 Captain Capron gave the command "Cannoneers, take your places." The sun was still hidden behind the high peaks of the Sierra Cobre, but there was light enough to see the general surroundings, while with a good glass one could distinguish the Spanish soldiers moving about the trenches which were lined thickly in front of the stone fort, and other men on horseback riding out of the fort. Capron's four pieces, which were of 3.2 caliber, were lined up at some little distance apart, but with their fire all concentrated on the fortifications. The range was announced to be from twenty-three hundred and fifty to twenty-four hundred yards. Just before the first gun was fired, and while comments were being freely made on the fact that no flag had been run up on the fort and surmises were being hazarded that the town had been evacuated, up popped the sun from behind the Sierra and up went the flag. Capron accepted this apparently as a defi, and immediately gave command to open the battle. He was the father of the young officer who had been killed at the skirmish of La Guasima, and it seemed fitting that he should have the honor of opening the assault on the city.

The first of our shells brought no answer, nor

did the next two or three, and the belief began to obtain that even if El Caney were not deserted there were no troops in it that would fight. Soon, however, an answer came in the shape of a Spanish shell, which burst on the roof of a small block house at one side of Capron's battery and in which a number of soldiers were standing to get a better view of the artillery duel. It wounded eighteen Americans and thirteen Cubans. This, however, was the best shot of the Spanish gunners for, while their line was moderately good, their range was generally too high. Capron's shooting was excellent, but though many of his shells struck the stone fort and a small block house which stood on another hill back of it, his guns were too light to cause any very great damage. At half-past seven the artillery fire on both sides slackened, but half an hour later Capron began his share of it again, with renewed energy, General Lawton's infantry being at that time prepared for its advance.

The same swale which lay between the bluff on which Capron's battery was placed and the hill on which the stone fort was perched extended around the suburbs in moderately well-defined fashion, but broken by rolling land and gullies and small winding streams; the general elevation of the country being lower to the left of the attack than it was to the right.

General Chaffee's Brigade began the infantry fight by moving along the extreme right over this higher ground. Then Ludlow's command began pressing across the low country to the left, both brigades moving forward in a series of rushes. The Spanish intrenchments stretched for a considerable distance to the right of the stone fort so that Chaffee's men were exposed to a heavy fire from the earthworks. The Spaniards, too, had thrown out sharpshooters all over the base and slope of the El Caney hill, and as our men dodged from cover to cover in single figures or rushed across a clear space in little groups, the men in the trenches fired by platoon and the sharpshooters picked off the advancing men.

For a long time, that is for what seemed to them a long time, Chaffee's men, while making their advance, had found themselves shot down and wounded by a fire that came from the left, and they had begun to imagine that they were exposed to Ludlow's fire from down the swale, when they discovered a masked, or rather, half-hidden blockhouse, on one of the spurs of the El Caney hill. It was found, too, to be a place of extreme strength against an infantry attack, being made of double thicknesses of pine planking with the intramural space filled with a lining of gravel and with earth heaped up around the base to a height of several feet, just above which embankment were narrow slits for the riflemen. Rifle pits also surrounded it, and around the rifle pits was a maze of barbed wire.

General Chaffee sent word to Captain Capron of the discovery of the block house and a fieldpiece was moved to a hillock where it could be trained on this Spanish pest hole, but the range was found to be too great, and as Chaffee's men at that time were swarming about the blockhouse, the cannon was called back. The taking of this blockhouse had occupied so much time that our men to the left had moved well forward to the edge of the swale before Chaffee was free, and the morning had, indeed, well advanced before the division occupied anything like a well-defined attacking line all around El Caney.

The Seventh was really the first regiment to get into commanding line; then came the Seventeenth, while, little by little, through groves of royal palms and mango trees, over slippery trails and by short cuts in the jungle; across gulches and through the high Cuban grass the Twelfth, Twenty-second, and Twenty-fifth got into line, then the Second Massachusetts, and so on, one regiment after another, until the long line of blue-shirted and brown-hatted men was stretched out, and the long-range rifle fight of Mauser against Krag-Jorgensen and Springfield was fairly on.

Foot by foot and rush by rush our men advanced closer and closer, while the fire from the Spanish trenches and fortifications grew heavier and heavier. The men mostly crept along on hands and knees, or wriggled from point to point, but the officers led their commands without any attempt at cover, and in this way did their share toward contributing to the great mortality among the leaders which characterized the campaign. As the Seventeenth, for instance, moved to close up the gap in the line between it and the Seventh, Lieutenant-Colonel J. H. Haskell led the way. It was across an open field, and as Haskell stepped out erect into the open space in the first line he fell. Lieutenant Dickinson ran ahead and was also fatally wounded. It was in the advance across this open country, too, that the men suffered most severely.

In fact, for the time, it was found impossible to further advance, and there the Seventh and Seventeenth lay under fire for about six hours. They poured their volleys into the Spanish breastworks, but apparently without effect; and, though the Spaniards could be plainly seen, something seemed to be wrong in our range, while the Spaniards were perfectly posted on the triangulation of every foot of land. The Springfield muskets of the Second Massachusetts were even more than ineffectual at this long-distance fight, and made so much smoke that twice they were ordered to cease firing. Close to the Second Massachusetts were lined out the Twelfth and Twenty-fifth regulars, but though by dint of incessantly dropping his shells on the fort Capron had succeeded in knocking out its corner bastions and rendering it comparatively innocuous, and though the fire of the Krag-Jorgensens was concentrated from all along our lines of regulars on the Spanish breastworks in a fierce continuous rattle, still the Spaniards kept up their volleys, while their Mauser bullets actually clipped off the grass tops which fell in showers on our men as though a mower were at work and chopped off twigs and branches in the trees above them as though a pruner were busy there. There seemed no possibility of cleaning out or silencing the trenches except by an advance in which decimation was the prospect, and as the hours wore on El Caney, which was to have been ours by a sharp and brilliant dash made before noon, was as bristling and defiant as ever. It was spoken of as "The Wasp's Nest," and well deserved its name.

But our men crept doggedly on and, when the long string of wounded made a continuous procession to the rear and the dead about them grew hourly in numbers, they only pressed on the fiercer. What at times changed the fierceness of our men to a condition of actual frenzy was when the sharpshooters who had crept through gaps in our lines or had been hidden in the trees before our advance was made, fired for very wantonness upon our wounded and upon the Red Cross men carrying them from the field. To be shot at themselves was what our men expected, because to shoot and to be shot was their business, but when the surgeons and hospital stewards toppled over, the volunteers fairly screeched with rage, while the regulars moved forward another foot and sent another bullet into the trenches.

Finally the swale was crossed and the attacking line was all around El Caney's hillside. Then it was seen that the chief source of our slaughter lay in a breastwork which had been run around the very edge of the village, extending from one building to another, with extensions at right angles down the slope of the hill. As has been said, the stone fort stood on a separate

hill with the village in a hollow beneath, and along the sides of this hill, too, trenches and breastworks had been run out at right angles so that shots from these could almost rake the whole length of our advancing line on the right.

Slowly our lines crept forward, and upward, regiment after regiment dashing across open spaces and seeking cover in the thickets which dotted the slopes of the suburb. When the term "regiment after regiment" is used it must not be understood as implying well-preserved regimental formation. Under the new condition of things, caused by the long-range rapid-fire weapons, it has been found wisest to scatter the forces so as not to subject troops to great loss by massing them, and at the same time to draw the fire of the enemy in a widely radiated direction. Even had not this new order of things been in existence as a codified plan of action, the nature of the ground over which our troops had to move here would have rendered even a battalion formation impossible. The Spaniards, it is repeated, knew the exact location of all the roads and paths and had the range perfectly, while our men as they advanced had to feel their way cautiously over rough and unfamiliar ground.

Bravely as the dashes were made it was bitter and deadly work for our men and officers. If our fighting was stubborn the resistance of the Spaniards was determined. Then, as though to add to the exactions of the day, at the very moment when things were at their worst at El Caney, the division commander at San Juan sent over to know if proceedings could not be hurried or abandoned so as to aid in the assault on San Juan. Before giving a reply, the courier from the center was taken down the line from Ludlow, on the extreme left, past Miles' brigade and Bates' independent brigade to Chaffee's position at the extreme right, all four brigades having been drawn into action by the tenacity of the defense. The proposition of virtually calling off his men and abandoning the results of a desperate half-day's work was laid before General Lawton, and he at once decided not to quit. Instead, and as though driven to desperation, word was sent all along the line that the trenches had to be taken and taken at once. And it was done in thirty minutes.

Captain Haskell, of the Twelfth Infantry, led the assault, his long white beard flying out behind him as he rushed forward. Far around to the left General Ludlow, with his white sailor hat stuck on the back of his head, galloped along the front and bade his men follow. His horse was killed under him, but afoot he pushed on,

The Fall of Santiago. 145

gloriously swinging his ridiculous little hat in his hand and still shouting to his men to come on. Two leaped out of cover and were shot down. The Twelfth and Twenty-fifth were almost deprived of their officers in the rush. Lieutenant McCorkle was killed and Captain Lawards and Lieutenant Murdock fell wounded, the disablement among the officers being so great that at one time Lieutenant Moss found himself commanding two companies. The Second Massachusetts struggled into the line of assault and Lieutenant Field was instantly killed. Lieutenant-Colonel Patterson, of the Twenty-second, was badly wounded and had to be sent to the rear, but there was no wavering among his men.

At last, after dodging from tree to brush and from brush to gully with Capron's guns banging away and the Spanish Mausers volleying incessantly, the first of the assaulting lines was actually formed under a group of trees at the foot of the hill. Then with a yell the troops, black and white and brown shot up the hillside, slashed down the wire fences and were in the trenches and had the fort. They were practically open graves and were filled with dead men.

Between the fort and the village stood a blockhouse, and as the living Spanish soldiers leaped out from among the dead Spanish soldiers in the trenches and made for the blockhouse, our men who were now swarming up over the ridge of the hill shot them as they ran, while those who had taken the fort joined in the slaughter.

Horrible as were the trenches the fort was as bad. As Captain Haskell, with Captain Clark just behind him, and their men pressing all around them, carried the fort, they found ample and awful evidence of the murderous work done by our fire and of the stubborn holding out against it. Out of the entire garrison but one Spanish officer and four men were alive. Seven lay dead in one small room and forty bodies were scattered along the shooting ways, the walls were shattered, the floors ran blood and the walls were splashed with it. Just as the fort was captured some fleeing Spaniard turned half-round and lodged a bullet in the arm of Mr. James Creelman. He, like Mr. Marshall, was a Journal correspondent, and like Mr. Marshall had esteemed it his duty to be in the thick of the fight.

With the fort and trenches in our possession the blockhouse was soon taken, and our men were scampering after the Spaniards as they fled down into the village. Of the Spaniards who had tried to seek shelter in the blockhouse as they ran from the trenches but few escaped, so deadly was the fire of our men as they steadied themselves after the rush up the hillside and brought down their men with the accuracy born of long target practice; and somehow or other when the blockhouse was reached nearly all of the Spaniards who had succeeded in getting into that shelter were found dead, victims to the bull's-eye accuracy of our men as they drove their Krag-Jorgensen bullets through the loopholes at the Spaniards behind them.

It was a weary set of men who found themselves victorious at the top of the El Caney hill, but there was lots of fight and fume in some of them yet, and these rushed into the town in order to bring down or round up a few more of the Spaniards. It was ugly work, for the town or village—and a pretty, quiet-looking village it looked from the top of the hill, with its red-tiled houses and mauresque church—proved to be a death trap. Its streets were festooned with barbed wire, the space between the pillars of the houses had been turned into forts by filling them breast high with stonework and across the roads had been placed barricades of fascines made by filling empty wine barrels with earth. But there was no fight left in the Spaniards now, and from houses and corners the soldiers crawled out in squads and surrendered to the number of one hundred and fifty-eight. So, with the afternoon sun well down was El Caney won.

The opposing forces, counting the relative character of the positions, were in number about equal. The Spaniards, with their usual power of minimizing defeat, claimed that the defense of El Caney was made by six hundred men, but it was later found that the garrison actually numbered over seventeen hundred men. But whatever their number, they fought to the death and held back Lawton for more than nine awful hours. It was nearly seven in the morning when Captain Capron fired his first gun, and it was five o'clock before El Caney fell.

The fighting had been hard and hot all day. Though there had not been much steady marching, our men had been alert, and on the move all the day under a broiling sun. The water in their canteens was soon consumed, and the hunt for streams and pools was a long and dolorous one.

The long-killing range of the Mauser rifle and the fact that the entire battlefield was the zone of fire was one of, if not the greatest, trial to the nerves of the men at El Caney. Troopers a mile behind our firing line were killed. As the Fourth Infantry, for instance, was marching to the aid of General Ludlow's Brigade, First Sergeant

After the capture of the El Caney Hill.—When the fastened fortress was taken the Spanish soldiers rushed down the hill toward the village, while the first of Lawton's men picked them off as they ran.

The Fall of Santiago. 149

Kirby was shot squarely through the heart although the distance from the front was over a mile. The consequence, apart from the trial to the spirit of the men which is the natural outcome of being killed by unseen enemies, was that when night came our dead and dying were scattered over the country for miles. The Spanish prisoners were set to work burying their own dead while the freshest of our men went back on the quest for their fallen comrades. The rest of the weary troops were gathered up as best they might be, and during the night they got about three hours of fitful napping. At night the Cuban support, which had done little more than scouting duty during the day, moved out to take a further position to the westward of Santiago, and all night long men who had lost their commands were straggling into the companionship of their companies, which for the moment meant their home. Capron's men threw themselves beside the guns which they had been working all day.

Then, notwithstanding all their fierce work on the previous day, when early morning came, General Lawton, leaving a garrison at El Caney, moved across country to help to strengthen Kent's line about San Juan.

If the American soldiers were impressed with

the desperate stubbornness of their Spanish opponents, it is also on record that the Spaniards were amazed at the brilliant courage of our men. One of the few surviving Spanish officers of the battle of El Caney, an aid on General Vara del Rey's staff, and present at the death of that officer, has related his impressions of the engagement. The narrative, which is told in the officer's own words, gives the Spanish view—somewhat fantastic in certain particulars—of one of the hardest-fought battles of the war. The narrator says:

"Brigadier-General Joaquin Vara del Rey, in command of the brigade of San Luis, composed of three companies of the Twenty-ninth regulars, numbering four hundred and sixty-seven men and forty-seven guerrillas, was ordered by General Linares to proceed from San Luis to Santiago, there to reinforce the garrison in the city.

"We left San Luis on June 23, marched to El Pozo, and thence to Santiago, where we stayed forty-eight hours, when we were ordered out to El Caney to strengthen the left flank of the Spanish lines. We arrived there on the 28th, in the evening, after an uneventful march.

"On the afternoon of the 30th we noticed a balloon ascending in the air, where it remained about a quarter of an hour. After its descent we saw the enemy pick up their tents and move their camp, but as the night was falling we were unable to locate their new position, although we guessed at it pretty correctly.

"We hurriedly dug trenches about three feet deep, in which the men fired kneeling.

"We worked at the trenches and breastworks all through the night, assigned the men to their posts and placed thirty regulars in the fort or blockhouse known as El Paraiso, fearing a surprise from the enemy.

"Our fears proved only too well grounded, for at daybreak the next morning, July 1, the first shell from the enemy's guns fell in the town.

"The Americans simultaneously opened with four rapid-fire guns and kept up a volcanic fire until three o'clock in the afternoon. We had no artillery with which to reply, and soon realized that we had the fight of our lives on our hands. All the ammunition we had was twelve mule loads of eight cases each.

"The enemy's fire was incessant, and we answered with equal rapidity. I have never seen anything to equal the courage and dash of those Americans, who, stripped to the waist, offering their naked breasts to our murderous fire, literally threw themselves on our trenches on the very muzzles of our guns.

"Our execution must have been terrible. We

had the advantage of our position and mowed them down by the hundreds, but they never retreated nor fell back an inch. As one man fell, shot through the heart, another would take his place with grim determination and unflinching devotion to duty in every line of his face.

"Their gallantry was heroic. We wondered at these men, who fought like lions and fell like men courting a wholesale massacre, which could well have been avoided had they only kept up their firing without storming our trenches.

"Our stock of ammunition was dwindling fast, we were losing rapidly, and were fighting the battle of despair, the inevitable staring us in the face. General Vara del Rey was standing in the square opposite the church when word was brought him that the last round had been served to the men. This was about three o'clock in the afternoon.

"He at once gave the order to retreat, crying to his men, 'Salvese quien pueda!'

"Hardly had he given the order before he fell shot through both legs. One of his aids, Lieutenant Joaquin Dominguez, turned to the general as he fell, exclaiming: 'General, what slaughter!' A bullet took the top clean off his skull, killing him on the spot.

"In the meantime I had secured a stretcher

The Fall of Santiago.   153

and ordered four men to place the general in it
and carry him to a place of safety. Bullets were
whizzing past us and falling like hail all around.
It seemed that fate was against us. As they
placed him in the stretcher General Vara del Rey
was shot through the head and killed.

"All four litter-bearers were shot and Lieutenant Antonio Vara del Rey, a brother and aid to
the general, was wounded and taken prisoner.
Earlier in the day Majors Aguero and Aragon,
both on the general's staff, had also been killed.
Beside these, ten other officers were shot, and
we had two hundred and thirty men killed and
wounded.

"At General Vara del Rey's death all took
flight, running down the hill and toward the
woods and underbrush, in a mad effort to get
away with their lives.

"Toward evening small bands of straggling,
worn-out soldiers began to arrive in Santiago,
and at half-past eight o'clock that night Colonel
Punet came in with one hundred and three men
whom he had been able to rally and bring into
the city in some sort of order.

"None of the blockhouses in the surrounding
country was engaged that day, but in the early
morning a shell from the American lines fell in

the San Miguel blockhouse, setting it on fire and killing seven men.

"We estimated the enemy's forces engaged at El Caney on July 1 at three thousand men and their artillery at four rapid-fire guns.

"It was the hardest fighting I have ever seen or ever care to see. The brilliancy and daring of the American attack was only equaled by the coolness and stubbornness of the Spanish defense.

"The report that the body of General Vara del Rey had never been recovered is untrue. It was buried by the American troops and his grave was marked with a wooden cross. A decoration found on his breast was unpinned and later handed to General Toral by General Shafter."

CHAPTER VIII.

HOW SAN JUAN WAS STORMED AND TAKEN.

THE first part of the battle of San Juan was a muddle; the second part was a glory.

Between the battles at El Caney and San Juan there were many salient points of similarity. In each case it was a fortified and intrenched hill that had to be attacked by our men; in each case the battle was opened with an artillery duel; in each case the difficulties of the country prevented the ready deployment of our troops, and in each case the fight was won by a dash of men in which individual grit more than compensated for the absence of brigade tactics or orders. In the case of San Juan, however, all of these factors were accentuated to an extraordinary degree.

San Juan hill is a veritable Gibraltar. It sharply rises a bare, rocky, steep-sided ridge from out—to preserve the figure of speech—a sea of meadow land which lies all around its base, except on that side which faces Santiago. This meadow land, locally called a 'Paradise,' is about a third of a mile wide and is broken in its expanse of tall entangling grass by these three objects: To the left, supposing one had marched up the road from Siboney, a small green knoll; to the right, a shallow pool or lagoon; between the lagoon and the road, another knoll somewhat higher than that to the left and surmounted by a pretty tiled-roof country seat. Looking at the San Juan hill from across the meadow land it would seem to be a clear rising, unbroken elevation, but a closer inspection of it would show that its surface was broken into a number of subsidiary ridges. On the topmost of these ridges was a large broad-eaved hacienda or farmhouse.

The commanding qualities of this farmhouse the Spanish engineers were quick to perceive, and the dwelling was easily transformed into a stronghold by piling up broken stone between the pillars of the piazza and by cutting loopholes in the walls of the house after the fashion found at El Caney and according to the plan generally described in the chapter dwelling on the march of the men to the front. Close to the house stood a shed and this also had been transformed into an improvised fort. Along the extreme crest of the hill, facing the meadow land, the Spanish engineers had dug a line of trenches in which the Spanish rifleman might stand and shoot down

Copyright by Mail and Express. Looking across the meadow land to the San Juan Hill. T
Rough Riders dashed in their assault.—To the l

...ier in the foreground is pointing to the lagoon across which the ...n a wind of the road from Siboney to Santiago.

any living thing that ventured to cross the 'Paradise' without any danger to himself. Back of the hacienda was a dip, then a rise, and on the top of this rise had been built one of the characteristic Spanish blockhouses, before which had been dug a second series of trenches. Still further back was another rise, another blockhouse and another series of trenches. Around and in front of the San Juan hacienda were strung entanglements of barbed wire; these were repeated before each of the lines of trenches to the rear, were strung across the face of the hill, stranded in the grass of the valley and stretched through the lagoon.

Let us now change our position as onlookers and stand on the San Juan hill, facing the road from Siboney. On the other side of the meadow land which swept round the base of the hill would be seen a broad expanse of jungle and thicket which closed in on the grassy level in a well-defined boundary far as the eye could reach. To the right the country was hilly, the nearest eminence being that of El Poso, on whose top was the home of a coffee planter. In an air line from the hacienda on the San Juan hill to that on El Poso hill the distance was, one would say, about two miles. To the left the wooded country sloped down to a moderate condition of plane, while in the distance were the ranges of the Sierra Cobre foothills, among whose mazes our men had marched up from the coast.

The lagoon was not the only water in the meadow land, for through it swept a bend of the winding San Juan River. This bend of the river could be traced for some distance to the right, would have to be crossed if a man were to walk direct from San Juan to El Poso, and turned into the woods in about what would be the center of the landscape. To the left of where the river thus turned into the woods and just back of the hill and blockhouse, spoken of just now as being one of the three breaks in the meadow land, the main road from the coast emerged. All about the exit point of the road the timber and vegetation grew so thickly that its line in the woods could not be distinguished. Once out in the meadow land the roadway was fairly plain, as it turned around the end of the lagoon and up the side of the San Juan hill, passing back of the hacienda toward Santiago.

If this description has been written clearly and has been followed closely the reader will see that the San Juan hill stood as a citadel in the path of those who passed to or from Santiago. It had to be taken before any advance could be made on the city. It was the Castilian lion in the path.

It will also be seen that in order to take the San Juan hill an advance would have to be made by regiments strung out along the road in the woods, and that, in order to attack the hill in anything like formation, the troops would have to debouch from the wood roadway and then deploy along the meadow land in the full face of the Spanish fire. It was a task before which a brave man might well recoil, and whose audacity appealed most strongly to the foreign military representatives present. These seeing what had to be done and what was done, wrote it down as an achievement of personal bravery before which the word impregnable was but an empty sound, and as one of the most astonishing examples of successful mistakes. In a word, it was the assault by infantry of a stronghold which should only have been reduced by artillery.

In meeting the problem thus presented to him, Brigadier-General J. Ford Kent, in command of the First Division, decided, naturally, that there were only two things to do—post what little artillery he had on El Poso hill, push his infantry as rapidly as possible up the road through the woods to the meadow land, and under partial cover of the artillery fire and the support of Lawton's men returning from El Caney, throw out his men into open order and carry the hill. This was done, though it was not done just as Kent had planned it should be. The troops in his division were these:

First Brigade, General Hawkins, Sixteenth and Sixth regulars and Seventy-first N. Y. V.

Second Brigade, General Pearson, Tenth, Twenty-first and Second, all regulars.

Third Brigade, General Wikoff, Ninth, Thirteenth and Thirty-fourth, all regulars.

Beside these he was assisted by General Wheeler's cavalry division, dismounted, consisting of the First, Ninth, and Tenth, regulars, and the Rough Riders.

The artillery was under charge of Captain Grimes, his battery going into position and preparing its gun-pits close to the ruins of the El Poso farmhouse on the night of June 30.

The morning was still and hot, hot with a tropical intensity, the meadow lands below being full of mist while the blue of the sky had a coppery tinge. The little dismantled ranch house with its tiled roof and rusted bell were just below Grimes' battery, and, barring this battery, the whole scene was as innocent as a picture. Not a man could be seen at San Juan, and there was not a sound from the right to indicate that up through the woods there was being pushed a long winding column of American soldiers. At twenty minutes to seven, Grimes, who had the bespectacled air of a professor, gave the command to fire, and our first shell went flying toward San Juan. Wherever it struck it did no damage and a few others were fired, not so much with a view of demolishing the fortified farmhouse as to find the enemy. He was found after ten shots, his answer coming in the shape of a muffled report from the hill and the hissing flight of a five-inch shrapnel shell which burst high in the air. It was a good line fire and the reserves were ordered into cover, but Grimes, like a very fierce professor now, kept his position and his command to "aim" and "fire" went on as steadily as the ticking of a sedate clock on a farmhouse stairway. So the give and take of the artillery part of the engagement proceeded until suddenly the Spanish fire ceased. But while it had lasted it had been deadly, for three of our artillerymen had been killed; three sergeants and a corporal of the battery had been wounded; in a dip under the hill twelve Cubans had been torn by the shrapnel, and in the wood road there had been terrible havoc. To that wood road it is now time to turn.

At nightfall of June 30 the three brigades bivouacked along the San Juan road around Sevilla. They were up by daybreak, and about the time when Grimes began his battery fire Hawkins, with the First Brigade, had reached that part of the road where it was crossed by the San Juan River, about two hundred and fifty yards to the right of El Poso hill. This river rises in the hills northeast of Santiago and follows a devious way under various local names down to the coast where it empties into the sea at Aguadores.

In its course its affluents cross the road from Siboney to San Juan several times, its course being so belooped in the neighborhood of San Juan that our troops had to ford it twice within a mile. The first of these crossings was that already referred to as being near El Poso, and the second was close up to the edge of the woods, where the forest ended and the meadow land began. Torrential stream as it is, it always carries a considerable body of water spread over the large area usually occupied by streams that are accustomed to sudden accessions and diminutions, being full of gravel bars and water pits. The river was really the road maker, for the road was drawn across the river wherever a ford was found.

Hawkins was moving smartly along the road and would have crossed both fords and have been at the debouche of the road into the meadow land had not the division commander (Kent) received orders from headquarters to give right of way to the cavalry which had been posted back of El Poso hill. The infantry was accordingly halted, and as the cavalry came up the road and also halted at the first ford when it got there, the first of the series of congestions which marked the gathering of the troops along the road thus took place. When the cavalry crossed the first ford and moved forward, Hawkins, seeing that his men were suffering severely from the Spanish fire, decided to move his men along as quickly as possible, and therefore ordered them to push alongside the cavalry, and this they did, so that Wheeler's division and the head of Hawkins' division were at this time marching in parallel lines, sometimes by file and sometimes two abreast. In such a movement of troops, even were the exigencies of travel alone to be considered, anything like distinct regimental segregation would soon have been imperiled; but when to these moving, crossing, mingling lines of men along a wood road were added the deadly and pestiferous attacks of the Spanish riflemen and artillerists, the impossibility of keeping the regiments distinct can readily be understood.

It had been expected, or at least hoped, that the attentions of Grimes' battery would keep the batteries and trenches at San Juan sufficiently employed to allow our men to advance up the road with only a moderate loss. The contrary was, however, the case and it was due principally to two causes—an experiment on our side and the Spanish sharpshooters.

If any point has been dwelt on in this history it has been that of attempting to show that the march from the sea to Santiago was for the most part through roads which were so bordered with forest and thickets of underbrush that, except when on an eminence, it was almost impossible to see beyond the turn of the road or to form any idea of what danger lurked in the tangles on either side. The consideration of hidden foes and attacks from ambush were always in the hearts of the men, if not always in the plans of the leaders. The same clever tactics and intimate local knowledge which were shown by the Spaniards at El Caney, La Guasima and Guantanamo were shown here with extreme emphasis. The Spaniards who knew that the San Juan hill commanded the way to Santiago knew also every foot of the region roundabout. They were aware of the natural obstacles to advance, the turns of the river and the sharp outlet on to the meadow land and to these natural obstacles had added the active fighting one of sharpshooters in the trees. It has been noted that this irregular branch of the service was found to be a favorite one with the Spanish strategy all during the Santiago campaign, but it was used with unusual freedom around San Juan.

Every tree from whose branches a turn of the road could be seen or guessed at seemed to hold a Spanish sharpshooter.

As these fellows used smokeless powder it was almost impossible to locate them by casual observation, and they had concealed themselves so cleverly in the foliage that it was sometimes impossible to discover them by close examination. As the Sixteenth and Sixth regiments of Hawkins' infantry and the cavalrymen of Wheeler's division were bunched together along the road about the fords, the sharpshooters in the trees reaped an awful harvest. The bullets kept chugging into our ranks and the men fell thickly here and there, and all at the hands of an absolutely invisible enemy.

Men were shot not only in front and flank, but from the rear, the fire being practically all around them. Not only were the losses serious, but the possible demoralization of the men was a still more serious matter, and two companies of colored troopers, whose regimental number need not be given, were at last ordered into the woods as pot hunters. They were told definitely that no prisoners were expected to be brought in; that every Spaniard found in a tree was to be killed. The order was a plain, swift necessity and the troopers set forward to carry it out with equal plainness and dispatch. They stalked from tree to tree and wherever the ping of a Mauser was heard or the flash of a rifle seen, the colored hunter bagged his game.

The term "brought down" his game can not be used for in many cases after the sharpshooter in the trees had been shot he did not fall. An investigation of this peculiar result showed that the Spaniard had been tied up in the tree. His Mauser would fall, but the man would not. It was found, too, that the sharpshooters were generally well supplied with provisions, so that the plan of those who tied the men in the trees to have them stay there for some time was clear, although it was never quite clear whether the men had been tied to the branches with their own consent or not. The story obtains, although it has not been proved, that in many cases the men were tied by order of the Spanish officers and so tied that they could not get down even had they wanted to. No particular question was asked of the pot hunters as to their success, but as they were away a long time, as they had much hunting ground to cover and as the fire of the sharpshoot-

From photograph by J. C. Hemment.   Copyright, 1898, by W. B. Hearst.
The balloon which drew the Spanish fire to the American troops massed along the road leading to San Juan, and which became known as "The Bloody Angle."

ers certainly grew markedly less, it is to be understood that the grim hints which the huntsmen brought back of ghastly fruit left to rot in many, many trees were founded on desperate but necessary fact.

Our experiment was that of a war balloon. It was in charge of the signal corps and was sent up under the care of Lieutenant Maxfield.

The ascension of the balloon resulted in a beneficial discovery and a catastrophe. The discovery was of a masked road or trail which led off to the left of the main road near the first ford and by following which a second way of reaching the open land could be had. The catastrophe was that the presence of the balloon was immediately divined by the Spanish leaders at San Juan to indicate the position of the troops and to show definitely that the Americans had reached the upper part of the road leading to the meadow land. Instantly, what shrapnel had been used in reply to Grimes' battery was deflected to the road, and every rifle in the trenches was pointed in the same direction. The sharpshooters' fire had diminished, it is true, but the hail of the shrapnel and the swarm of Mauser bullets was worse. The killing power of the Spanish rifle at long range was never more distinctively felt than at this time. It was a long-distance fight with a vengeance, but it was one in which our men had to stand and take without being able to deliver a reply.

The discovery of the branch road was utilized as speedily as possible. The first regiment to be sent up to the left from the front was the Seventy-first New York Volunteers. By sending it up this trail, the regiment was at once separated from the rest of the brigade, the other two regiments, the Sixteenth and Sixth, both regulars, it must be remembered, being at that time engaged in squeezing and pushing its way forward as a parallel line to the cavalrymen of Wheeler's brigade. Between the volunteer regiment and the regiments of regulars lay the woods and thickets, not yet cleared of sharpshooters. The garrison on San Juan hill either knew from observation, or inferred, that the secondary road was being utilized, for no sooner had the first battalion of the Seventy-first started up the branch road than to the fire of the sharpshooters was added whatever shrapnel and rifle volleys from the trenches were not given to the men in the main road.

The report of the division commander when dealing with this part of the day states that no sooner had the First Battalion of the Seventy-first been turned into this byway with orders to march up it and form so as to get into line with the other two regiments of the division, than "it was exposed to such a galling fire that it recoiled in confusion on the rear." This is Kent's cold-blooded official statement and there can be no doubt as to its accuracy. Neither can there be any doubt as to the utter absence of anything like an extenuating or explanatory statement in the division commander's report. No reference whatever is made to the fact that by thus ordering the volunteers up a side road, unsupported by regulars, they were at once thrown into a position of the most unusually trying character. It was not even a regimental advance, but the stringing out of a battalion along a narrow road, where every step meant possible death. It is true that this is the sort of thing that all soldiers, whether volunteers or regulars, are expected to encounter; but it is also true that this exposure of an unsupported battalion of volunteers was one of marked severity. Due emphasis may be laid upon these conditions, it is believed, without in the faintest advancing anything in the nature of a special plea.

The First Battalion was ordered to lie down, and it did so, and, by the bye, it was one of the crying faults of the volunteers in the whole Santiago campaign that they did not lie down as much as they should have done to escape the

Spanish fire. The regulars knew that seeking cover did not imply cowardice; the volunteers were afraid that it did. While the First Battalion was lying down, the Second and Third came steadily along and moved up the trail.

At twenty minutes past twelve the Third Brigade, Wickoff's, reached the forks, and was sent forward by the left road, up which it marched, pushing forward past the volunteers and so to the edge of the woods. No sooner had the Third Brigade been thus disposed of than up came the Second Brigade (Pearson's), forming the rear. This brigade was split at the forks, the Tenth and Second Regiments being sent up the trail to the left and the Twenty-first along the main road. In each case the different regiments were instructed to form with their fellow regiments of the same brigade when possible. But by thus splitting the forces it came about that only in the case of the Second was anything like a brigade formation preserved. The troops stood in this wise:

UP THE BRANCH ROAD.
First Brigade:
  Seventy-first New York Vol.
Third Brigade:
  Ninth.
  Thirteenth.
  Twenty-fourth.
Second Brigade:
  Second.
  Tenth.

UP THE MAIN ROAD.
Wheeler's Cavalry:
  First.
  Tenth.
  Ninth.
  Rough Riders.
First Brigade:
  Sixteenth.
  Sixth.
Second Brigade:
  Twenty-first.

The Fall of Santiago.   171

When the Third Brigade reached the edge of the wood it found itself at a ford of the San Juan River, which in its erratic course had turned that way. Wickoff saw that the only way to save his men from annihilation in crossing the stream and gaining the open was to deploy and rush for it. Word was given to this effect, was passed along the line, and with a cheer everybody along the road started in on one of those dashing rushes which characterized the day. Through the jungle, across the stream knee-high, waist-high, and up and over its banks—slippery with the mud of the bottom lands and tangled with barbed-wire—across the shingle beds into which the feet slipped, the men rushed. Even the division commander acknowledges that in this wild dash for the open there was nothing approaching brigade formation. By companies, here and there, battalions now and then, and by regiments rarely, the Third Brigade, gathering up as it went the foremost of the Seventy-first New Yorkers, with Captain Goldsborough of Company M acting as their impromtu major, reached the open and actually formed into something like a well-defined line of assault. But it was bloody work.

Wickoff was killed as he ran ahead, keeping the men together. Lieutenant-Colonel Worth of the Thirteenth took his place, and went down severely wounded. Lieutenant-Colonel Liscum of the Twenty-fourth, upon whom the brigade command then descended, took up the lead with a cheer which had scarcely begun when he too fell, and as the brigade swept up to the hill it was under charge of Lieutenant-Colonel E. P. Ewers of the Ninth. Those who from the woods could see the burst of the Third Brigade and its lightning formation and dash across the open have said that it was one of the most brilliant and stirring things ever seen on a battlefield. It only lasted ten minutes, but in those ten minutes the brigade command had thrice descended on the field, while the brigade men lay scattered in pitiful numbers all over the Paradise.

If the jam and congestion of men in the main road had been confusing while the two regiments of the First Brigade and Wheeler's dismounted cavalrymen were struggling for the right of way, it can be imagined what the congestion and jam were like when the regiments of the other brigades were added to the mass of men. The deflection of part of the troops into the trail on the left was what might literally be called an avenue of relief, but, even with this, the two roads for miles back from the open were full of crowded columns of men all in more or less disorder, all exposed to a deadly fire which lasted all through the morning hours and all anxiously waiting for a chance to get out and kill something they could see or be killed by a visible enemy. To the layman the simple solution of the whole matter would, perhaps, seem a steady march along the roads and a quick burst into the open of each company as it arrived at the meadow land, the rapid deploy of those who emerged and the continuous accession to the deploy line of men from behind. In such a clearance of the congestion many would surely fall, but some would surely escape, enough, anyway, to form a good line of advance. But to the military leaders no such simple method of relief was found practicable, or, at any rate, it was not put into practice. Indeed, to the men in the woods, it looked as though the military leaders did not exactly know what to do, and in the same cold-blooded spirit of telling facts which characterizes Kent's report, it must be stated that on a quiet after consideration of the battle the surviving brigade and regimental commanders were of the very decided, if altogether unofficial, opinion that the day had been remarkable for its utter absence of either brigade or regimental orders received and carried out.

Orders were issued which, if strictly obeyed, would have meant that some regiments would be still waiting in the San Juan road; and in other cases contradiction traveled so quickly on the heels of orders, and reaffirmations so quickly on the heels of contradictions, that sometimes the order of the dispatches was mixed and a regimental commander was dutifully undoing that which he was expected to be performing.

But of it all the Third Brigade, as has been said, did burst out into the open and, as it did so, the two regiments of Hawkins' brigade (the Sixteenth and Sixth) also broke from the mass of men at the head of the main road.

The Third and First brigades were out, and those who stood on the top of El Poso hill and saw this burst of men said that the efflux of scampering, dodging, cheering men was like that of the frothy spume of champagne from two bottle necks. Almost at the same time, for chronological accuracy in such details as minutes seemed absolutely impossible in the face of the general and undefined advance, the cavalry division leaped free of the woods and made a dash for the hillock which has been described as occupying a point in the meadow land between the lagoon and the woods. With them, or after them, or close on the heels of Hawkins' regiments ran the Twenty-first regiment of Pearson's Second Brigade, while far to the left his other two regiments, the Tenth and Second, which were to the rear of Wickoff's brigade in the branch or path also broke cover and swept out behind the grassy knoll which has been described as occupying a point in the airline between El Poso and San Juan hills. These two regiments furnished a notable exception to the general method of advance, and did actually move forward in company to the rear of the knoll. There they deployed and advanced in a line over its crest and into the meadow, which, now as far as the eye could reach, was alive with blue-shirted soldiers with their faces all turned one way—to the San Juan hill.

What does it matter who got there first? The division commander confesses his inability to say, and the one incontrovertible fact is that the Sixth and the Sixteenth on the right, the Ninth, Thirteenth and Twenty-fourth, and the fighting battalions of the Seventy-first New York Volunteers all got to the top of the hill about the same time, and that the leading men were there at some minute between 1:25 and 1:30 p. m. A simple statement this, made as the result of a dissection of varying reports in the search for truths, but covering a collection of stirring deeds such as will be to the history of the American soldier what that of Tel-el-Kebir is to the British.

The battle of San Juan has been called a battle of squads; it was really a battle of men. It was not the *esprit du corps*, though that existed, which carried the day; it was the *esprit d'homme*. Out where the Sixth and Sixteenth were plunging forward, had the day depended on orders, it would have been a disaster instead of a victory. Captain Kenon, Company E, of the Sixth, and Captain Byrnes, Company F, had got out and were lining forward when the two met a company of the Sixteenth, merged and went on again, without any company division. Kenon and the men who followed him, went up the hill in a flanking way, then turned at right angles to face the first blockhouse. When he reached the top and turned he was alone. His men had taken another line of attack, and when the regiment behind him came piling up it proved to be Byrnes' men, or, at least, a much-mixed lot who were following Byrnes. Kenon and Byrnes shook hands, mutually congratulating each other on being the first to reach the summit, when there was a cheer to the left, and Lieutenant Ord was seen leaping across the trenches with a file of men behind him. Ord was a staff officer, but had joined the firing line, and in the climb up the hill had gathered a promiscuous lot of soldiers whose regimental numbers included almost everything on the field.

The Fall of Santiago. 177

When the Sixth and Sixteenth started from the woods Hawkins placed himself between the two regiments and cheered his men along, and when he panted to the top and was cheered by his men, there were as many of Wickoff's troopers about him as of the regiments he had led.

Even in the assault on the trenches, and the confusion which followed it, the men on the hill could hear the yell of the Rough Riders and colored troopers as they, too, rushed down the slope of the hill on which stood the blockhouse, which they had assaulted and carried, and trotted and pulled themselves up the San Juan hill to be in at the death. General Wheeler, sick and almost sunstruck though he was, had stuck to his division in the "Bloody Angle" and struggled forward to watch the charge of his horsemen on foot. He saw the lightning fall of the blockhouse, and as he saw it the memorable but most forgivable mistaken cry escaped him of "There go the Yankees. Give it to 'em, boys!" Between the blockhouse hill and the main San Juan hill lay the lagoon, and through it the Rough Riders dashed, Colonel Roosevelt splashing and cheering at the head of his men.

This is what our men had been doing. Meanwhile, as the charge was made across the open and up the hill, the Spaniards turned their volleys on the advancing troops. It was a withering fire before which the men reeled and dropped in their tracks. As though by a common impulse, our men refrained from firing until they were close upon the trenches, and indeed until they could see the men individually in the rifle-pits. Blue-shirted men lay in hundreds over the thick grass, in the shallow waters of the pool, and on the slopes of the hill—slopes so steep that in many cases the men had to pull themselves up by rocks and bushes. At last they could see the enemy, see the whites of their eyes, and then steadying themselves, the whole army pumped American bullets into the Spanish line. The first line of trenches was a shambles, and throwing out the dead Spaniards, our men dropped into the horrible slime and directed their fire on the enemy, now running pellmell to the second line of defense.

But, though the first line was gained, and the second was commanded by our position in the first line of trenches, the Spaniards as yet showed no disposition to acknowledge the day as lost. A hurried council of war was called in a break beneath the brow of the hill, and it was decided to rush and carry the other trenches and blockhouses. After the work of the morning this was comparatively easy, that is, it was a plain case of

From photograph by J. C. Hemment.
The Seventy-first N. Y. Volunteers as they were turned into the by-path off the main road
it was while the Seventy-first were marching up the by-path that they

Copyright, 1898, by W. B. Hearst.

an Juan. The two regular regiments of the Brigade were up the road to the right, and met by what the Division Commander styled "a withering fire."

fight. The charge was led by Roosevelt at the head of the Rough Riders and the Twenty-fourth Colored, and tired as the men were, they formed behind the hacienda and swept on irresistibly. This was fighting work they could do and feel moderately at home in. It was not the lurking hidden death which they had been facing from eight until noon. There were the trenches and the blockhouses on the rolling lands before them. By rush and volley they went and by volleys from the trenches they were met. It was awful work, but there was the fever of fight in the men, and by 3:50 P. M. the last intrenchment was carried and the Spaniards had retired to the outworks of Santiago.

The men who carried the trenches remarked on the great number of Spanish dead, and it was the general opinion that out of those whose volleys made such frightful holes in the advancing Americans, from seventy to eighty-five per cent. went down in that terrible hail of bullets sent in by our men when they had a fair chance to show their deadly accuracy of aim. The chief loss was the disabling of General Linares, who was shot by Sergeant McKinnery, of Company D, Ninth Infantry, at a thousand yards. Linares immediately relinquished the command to General Toral, nor did he again assume it pending the campaign.

It was a glorious victory, but dearly bought. Every regiment had lost and lost heavily. Twelve officers and seventy-seven men killed, and thirty-two officers and four hundred and sixty-three men wounded made up the casualties to the First Division, the official report in detail being as follows:

REPORT OF KILLED, WOUNDED AND MISSING, FIRST DIVISION, FIFTH ARMY CORPS, JULY 1, 1898.

Organization.	Killed.		Wounded.		Missing.
	Officers.	Men.	Officers.	Men.	
First Brigade:					
Sixteenth Infantry..................	1	13	5	82	6
Sixth Infantry.....................	4	13	7	95	.....
Seventy-first N. Y. Vol. Infantry....	.....	12	1	47	43
Totals..........................	5	38	13	224	49
Second Brigade:					
Tenth Infantry.....................	1	4	5	21	.....
Twenty-first Infantry...............	.....	5	1	25	.....
Second Infantry....................	.....	1	4	16	.....
Totals..........................	1	10	10	62	.....
Third Brigade:					
Brigade Commander	1	.....	.....	.....	.....
Ninth Infantry.....................	1	3	.....	23	1
Thirteenth Infantry	2	16	5	81	1
Twenty-fourth Infantry.............	2	10	4	73	7
Totals..........................	6	29	9	177	9
Grand totals.......................	12	77	32	463	58

It was at 4:45 p. m. that the firing died away —a firing which had been terrific, and so the foreign expert observers said, unexampled in its fierceness and intensity—and quiet fell on the valley, a quiet so sudden and startling that it seemed as though the machinery of the universe had stopped running. It was a case of actual exhaustion on both sides, and though it was known afterward that had the Americans pursued their advantage they could have followed the Spaniards clear into Santiago and have taken it almost without a struggle, we could not have done so even if it had required no more exertion than driving into the city a flock of sheep. The men dropped where they stood, and all they knew or cared for was that they had won the battle of San Juan, and that the impregnable Gibraltar of the Santiago highroad was theirs.

Though the San Juan hill was taken Santiago was by no means ours. After trench-digging and the early morning visit of the commissariat it was hoped that a few hours' sleep might be granted our men, but such was not the Spanish idea. At five o'clock on Saturday morning the enemy made a desperate effort to recover its lost position. Again and again the hill was assaulted and again and again the Spanish soldiers were driven back—driven back too, with awful losses

—for now the conditions were reversed. Our men were intrenched and the Spaniards were attacking an intrenched position. The dynamite gun of the Rough Riders did telling work throughout the day, throwing shells into Santiago itself, and a battery of Hotchkiss guns was set up near the hacienda and cut swathes out of the enemy's ranks.

All day long the assaults of varying determination were made and night, that is, the night of Saturday, July 2, brought a general sortie. It was at 9:30 that the firing of the pickets brought the wearied men once more to their feet. The Spaniards swarmed through the outer lines and pushed their way desperately on until in many cases they reached within a hundred yards of our lines. But in the trenches now stood men whose fire was cool and deadly, the sortie was completely repulsed and the Spaniard fell back to his third line which placed him close under the walls of Santiago. Next morning, however, the Spaniards were again at it, but in a desultory long-distance firing which lasted until noon, when, to the surprise of those who did not know of the curious things that were happening at headquarters, a flag of truce was displayed and the order to cease firing ran along the lines.

Owing to the reversal of positions just spoken

of, our losses at San Juan in the second and third day's fighting were trifling compared to what they had been on the first. Nine men killed, four officers and ninety men wounded, made up the casualties of July 2; while in the third day's fighting only one man was killed and eight were wounded.

In the three days' fighting the losses were as follows:

	At San Juan.		At El Caney.		Total.	
	Officers.	Men.	Officers.	Men.	Officers.	Men.
Killed............	12	87	11	121	23	208
Wounded.........	36	561	44	642	80	1,203
Missing..........		62		19		81
	48	710	55	782	103	1,492

While it was and has been difficult to secure anything like a definite statement of the Spanish casualties, the following figures are substantially correct. At El Caney the killed, wounded and prisoners were found in round numbers to have been two thousand. At San Juan they reached three thousand, a total of killed, wounded and prisoners of five thousand.

It was said just now that the display of the white flag was a surprise to those who saw it and who were not acquainted with the strange things that had happened at headquarters. This is the record: General Shafter, who, during the triple fight of July 1, had been lying sick at Sevilla, was in a much worse physical condition on July 2, while to his bodily ailments was added much mental perturbation. From the reports brought him from the front he learned of El Caney's stubborn resistance, of the slaughter at San Juan, of the Spaniard's persistent fighting at this latter place and of the small things done at Aguadores by Brigadier-General Duffield. With the Thirty-third Michigan Volunteers, a battalion of the Thirty-fourth Michigan and about two thousand Cubans this officer, it will be remembered, was to advance on the little fortified town at the mouth of the San Juan River. Aguadores, with its four thousand Spanish troops, was to be shelled by the New York and Suwanee while Duffield engaged them in a shore attack or cut off their escape to Santiago. But when Duffield neared Aguadores he found that the Spaniards had destroyed the railroad trestle across the San Juan, the Michigan men being obliged to halt on this side of a ravine, and that the bombardment by the flagship and her consort had done no material damage to the fort. When Duffield's men appeared, the fort opened fire and with its first

Where Duffield was held in check outside Aquadores July 1.—The trestle was dynamited by the Spanish engineers, and Duffield's men were exposed to such a heavy fire from the Spanish forts on the other side of the ravine that they had to retire.

three shells killed twenty-three Cubans and two men of the Thirty-third. Duffield replied with a few volleys, but seeing the hopelessness of his position retired along the Siboney road.

Learning of these things Shafter, on Saturday, called a council of war, during which the proposition was advanced whether it would not be better to retire the American army to the high lands above Siboney pending the arrival and emplacement of heavy siege guns. Generals Kent and Sumner, who had arrived from San Juan, favored a withdrawal, but General Wheeler said bluntly that he proposed to stay where he was and in this stand he was backed by Generals Lawton and Bates, who came in from El Caney. Shafter's depression was so great, however, that he did not abandon his idea of retiring but determined, with a full appreciation of the gravity of such a movement, that the American lines should meanwhile be thrown as far north as possible. And, with a policy of contingencies that was most remarkable and that produced still more remarkable results, he decided to demand the surrender of Santiago. In this remarkable determination General Shafter anticipated that, under cover of the negotiations that would certainly follow such a demand, he might be able to retire with safety and dignity and it may be, although it is not on record, that the wild hope may have been entertained that the commander of the Santiago forces would be surprised by such a demand into actual surrender. It is on record, however, that the government at Washington received on Sunday, July 3, two dispatches from Shafter which by turns so quickly depressed and elated it and which for a time seemed so inexplicable in their contradiction that they still occupy a prominent place in the documentary wonders of the campaign. The first dispatch was as follows:

"PLAYA DEL ESTE, July 3. To Secretary of War, Washington. Camp near Sevilla, Cuba, July 3. We have the town well invested on the north and east, but with a very thin line. Upon approaching it we find it of such a character and the defenses so strong it will be impossible to carry it by storm with my present force.

"Our losses up to date will aggregate a thousand, but the list has not yet been made. There is but little sickness outside of exhaustion from intense heat and exertion of the battle of the day before yesterday, and the almost constant fire which is kept up on the trenches.

"SHAFTER, Major-General."

The effect of this dispatch upon the government was as depressing as was its tone. A general council of war was called for and held at noon in the office of the Secretary of War, at which it was decided to rush all possible reinforcements to Shafter, to send him a message of gratitude and thanks; while the conclusion was reached that the results before Santiago were those of a drawn battle and the expectation was entertained that the next news from Shafter would be that he had abandoned El Caney and the San Juan plateau and was preparing to move his troops to the Siboney highlands for rest and preparation. Alger sent a dispatch of comfort to the effect that the President directed him to forward "the gratitude and thanks of the nation for the brilliant and effective work" of the Santiago army on July 1. General Miles sent his congratulations and the notice that he expected to be with him (Shafter) "within one week with strong reinforcements."

Following close on the receipt of Shafter's pessimistic report and the dispatch of the government's message of comfort came, like a sudden sun ray through a rift in a dark cloud, this remarkable dispatch:

"PLAYA DEL ESTE, July 3. To Secretary of War, Washington. Camp near Sevilla, Cuba, July 3. I sent a demand for the immediate surrender of Santiago, threatening to bombard the city. I believe the place will be surrendered. The following is my demand for the surrender of Santiago:

" 'Commanding General Spanish forces, Santiago de Cuba, July 3.

" 'I shall be obliged, unless you surrender, to shell Santiago de Cuba. Please inform the citizens of foreign countries and all women and children that they should leave the city before ten o'clock to-morrow morning.'

"Very respectfully, SHAFTER,
"Major-General Commanding."

But Washington had not yet done with the surprises to which Shafter was to treat it on the momentous Sunday, July 3. Prior to the report from the General of his demand for the surrender of Santiago and his announcement that he believed that the command would be complied with, the government had received an intimation from Colonel Allen, in command of the cable station at Playa del Este, that the Spanish fleet "had been destroyed and was burning on the beach." What "beach" or how "destroyed" this first and meager information of a great event did not say. Then came this dispatch from Shafter:

"Headquarters Fifth Army Corps,
"Cuba, July 3.
"The Spanish fleet left the harbor this morning and is reported practically destroyed. I demanded the surrender of the city at ten o'clock to-day. At this hour, four-thirty P.M. no reply has been received. Perfect quiet along the line.

The situation has been precarious on account of the difficulties of supplying the command with food and the tremendous fighting capabilities shown by the enemy, who has almost an impregnable position.

"SHAFTER, Commanding."

The American Army was ready to fall back; the demand for Santiago's surrender had been made and would be complied with; the Spanish fleet had been destroyed; and the demand for the city's surrender was still being considered— it was a combination of contradictory and sensational news which left the Government still guessing and which set the public agape.

From this confusion, and the presentation of its existence is necessary in a story which aims at accurately presenting the condition of things both at home and abroad, it is pleasant to turn to the facts of events.

CHAPTER IX.

HOW SCHLEY DESTROYED CERVERA'S FLEET.

Except in a casual way it has not been found necessary, in the progress of this history, to refer to Cervera's fleet from the moment of its discovery inside Santiago Harbor by Schley. The fleet was there, shut up in the land-locked harbor; the subject of forcing the passage, braving the mines and risking the fires of the batteries and engaging the fleet had, as has been told, formed the subject of conversation and plan between Admiral Sampson and his commanders; and the Merrimac, as has also been told, was sunk partly athwart the channel by Hobson —but outside of these facts and references Cervera's fleet has been a passive factor in this story.

It will be remembered that when the great running Admiral got behind the shelter of El Morro and La Socapa his seclusion was entitled by the Spanish authorities "a great tactical victory," while our authorities were equally precise in esteeming the process of bottling it up as the settlement of an undefined danger. But, housed as it was in Santiago Harbor and partially locked though the door might be, Cerverva's fleet was still in existence and sometime or other would have to be met and accounted for. As to how that meeting would occur there were many surmises, but not even the deftest romancer in the fleet ever spun a yarn so full of bright and glowing threads as that in which Cervera was moored, wound up and ended. The spectacular element, of whose profusion in this campaign I have before remarked, was eminently, distinguishingly present in the last act of Cervera's appearance in the rôle of naval commander.

Passive though the Spanish fleet may have seemed to be in its imprisonment, the time had been by no means one of inaction to the Spaniards. To the contrary, it had been one in which movement and anxiety had had equal parts.

The story of Cervera's imprisonment, and attempt to escape as told by the Spaniards themselves is rather a pitiful one. Those who tell it are Captain Eulate of the Viscaya, Captain Contreres of the Colon, Carinz the impressed and official pilot of the Spanish fleet, and, lastly, that log of the Colon out of which we have already gathered the story of Cervera's flitting from port to port. It is a long story as well as a pitiful one, but some of it must be told here.

The time of feasting and frolic which followed the entrance of Cervera's fleet into Santiago Harbor on May 19th lasted until the appearance on the outside of Schley's grim-looking warships. Then the rollicking was cut short, shore-leave cut off and feverish activity took their place. Just as our naval commanders were busy in devising plans to keep Cervera from coming out, so Cervera was hard at work devising plans to keep Schley and Sampson from coming in. Four six-inch guns were taken out of the Reina Mercedes, two of them placed in La Socapa battery so as to enfilade the neck of the harbor and two mounted in a shore battery opposite Cay Smith; the electric mines in the channels were reinforced with a number of contact mines; a great boom of logs and swinging rope nooses was laid clear across the bay between the entrance and the fleet, and four rapid-fire six-pounders were removed from the flagship and placed in shore earthworks opposite the narrowest part of the entrance. When all of these works of protection had been done, and their accomplishment occupied until May 31, both Cervera and Linares held that Santiago was impregnable to a sea attack and indeed it seemed a peculiar fancy of the Spanish commanders that they were always contriving and constructing "impregnable" positions, with the equally nugatory result that the "impregnable positions" were always either carried by the enemy or abandoned by themselves.

Hobson learned something of the nature of Santiago's defenses and much more was learned afterwards by Schley when he made the tour of the batteries after the surrender of the city, but it is evident that Hobson did not know all, and that Schley was rather inclined to judge superficially. Hobson saw nothing but what he was allowed to see, and Schley only saw what the Spaniards had left in the way of visible defenses. It is from the Spanish revelations of what had been done to guard Cervera's fleet against attack that we gain an exact idea of what our fleet would have had to encounter had it pressed into the harbor to atack the Spaniard.

When the American army landed at Daiquiri and Siboney, two gun crews were sent from each Spanish ship with three-pounder landing guns and a battery of automatic guns to assist the Spanish forces. Guns and men took an active part in the battles of El Caney and San Juan, two of the officers and many of the men being killed there. When both of these strongholds were taken the desperate nature of the situation appealed so strongly to both Cervera and Linares that the latter sent an almost despairing message to Blanco who replied, as Governor General of Cuba, by ordering Cervera to make a run for it. On the receipt of these instructions Cervera, on the afternoon of July 2, signalled his captains to a conference at which it was agreed by all the commanders, except those of the torpedo-boat destroyers, that it was best to make the attempt to escape at night. The American troops were pressing forward, taking line after line of intrenchments; Shafter's indecision and fears were not known of, and the American fleet seemed to be closing in on the harbor, so it was decided to go out that very night at eleven o'clock. As soon as darkness set in the preparatory work for the dash into the open sea was begun. The contact mines, lying to the west of the Merrimac, were removed, the big boom was drawn aside and the ships were massed near the entrance. But night brought no relaxation of vigilance on the part of the American blockaders. To the contrary, it was seen that the blockading fleet was drawn up in unusually close lines, the great white cones of the flash-lights played uninterruptedly on the entrance; while up on the hills beacon fires were burning. To Cervera and his officers it appeared impossible to get away from this wary, watchful

The Fall of Santiago. 195

foe and when he ran up the querulous signal, "Do you think we had better wait until daylight," all the captains answered "Yes."

The Spanish ships were then withdrawn up the harbor, the boom thrown back, the contact mines replaced and daylight waited for. But when daylight came and the ships once more steamed down to the entrance, there lay the blockading fleet close and wary as ever. Fires were all going in the Spaniards' boiler rooms, and at nine o'clock the captains and admirals met for a final conference. It was decided that no more delay was possible, and that the only thing left was to get up all steam possible and, as soon as a fourteen knot power was made, to start. The order of the ships' exits were set in this wise: First the Infanta Maria Teresa, with Cervera on board; then the Viscaya, then the Almirante Oquendo, then the Cristobal Colon, each with a cable's length headway. It was planned that the three first named were to engage the enemy running and that the Colon, as the fleetest of the cruisers and under cover of this engagement, was to put on full speed to the west and get away to Cienfuegos. Most of the baggage and valuables of the officers was put on board the Colon, for while the upshot of the fight between the Teresa, Viscaya and Oquendo and our ships was in doubt, none was entertained as to the ability of the Colon to outstrip her pursuers. The gunboat destroyers were to follow the Colon and aid in covering the escape of that ship.

The swift-running, heavy-batteried Brooklyn was the most dreaded of the American ships and all the Spanish captains were instructed to make a joint attempt to sink her, every big gun being trained forward of the beam so that on emerging from the entrance all would be aimed at her. While these last instructions were being given, the signalman at El Morro announced that the American flagship had just left for the East and that the Newark and Massachusetts were also well down the coast. It seemed to the Spaniards as though Providence was on their side at last, the captains were hurried to their ships and the dash for liberty was begun.

The lookout on El Morro had correctly reported. The joint attack on Santiago by the land and sea forces, as an emphatic aid to hasten a capitulation, was to be arranged, and Sampson steamed down early on this Sunday morning to Siboney for the purpose of consulting with Shafter. As the New York turned eastward she flew the signal "Disregard commander-in-chief's movements." Her departure left Schley in virtual command of the blockading fleet and so it happened that, because of this Sunday morning visit, it was left for Schley to carry out those laconic instructions which he had received from Washington when he reported his discovery of Cervera's fleet. He had been told to "capture or destroy" the Spanish ships and he did so. Admiral Sampson's departure for the confabulation at Siboney did not, it is true, shift the command; he was still commander-in-chief of the fleet, and officially was at the head of the American war vessels when they shot and smothered Cervera's lean cruisers out of existence. But, while officially present, he was personally absent and to the plain people, who so stubbornly stick to plain facts and pocket official fictions, it was Schley, Schley and his fighting fellow-commanders to whom is due the glory of the battle of July 3d.

No one doubts the ability and foresight of Rear Admiral Sampson. After the landing of the army of invasion Sampson instructed his captains to "maintain and display the utmost vigilance in guarding the harbor entrance." This was specifically enjoined on them and they were as specifically told that "if the Spanish admiral ever intends to try to escape he will make that effort now." That possibility was emphatically laid down and the commanders understood and appreciated the wisdom and foresight of their chief.

But the night was always regarded as the time when Cervera would, in all probability, make his running. The cover of darkness and the confusion of a night battle were always considered the elements which Cervera would choose as aids to his escape and, while it cannot be said that nobody dreamed Cervera would bolt for it in full daylight, certainly such a possibility could not have been seriously considered by Sampson or he would not have left the fleet on this Sunday morning. As Cervera had found on the preceding night, the American lines were closely drawn about the entrance and the searchlights lit up every inch between the heights of El Morro and La Socapa. But when morning dawned the lines of the blockading squadron were broken. Of the flagship's whereabouts we know. The battleship Massachusetts early in the morning had gone to Guantanamo; the Marblehead was also at that base of supplies; the New Orleans had been sent to Key West and of the numerous auxiliary fleet two only, the converted yacht Gloucester and the converted tugboat Vixen, were left on blockade—the others being widely scattered along the coast from Guantanamo to Acerradores.

We know what the Spaniards had been doing, what preparations they had made and how they were lined up behind the shelter of the entrance

The Fall of Santiago.   199

cliffs waiting for the signal to run; let us now see how lay that part of the American squadron which remained on blockade duty.

The morning was clear and a painter would have said that the sea was turquoise and that the sky from zenith to horizon was shaded from sapphire to topaz. The American ships lay in a long semicircle, with its distance from the shore ranging from about two miles at the horns of the crescent to about five miles in the fullness of the bow. The little Vixen lay at the western horn of the crescent, she being close under the hills at Cabañas; a mile to the eastward and outward lay the Brooklyn flying Commodore Schley's flag; next, and at equal distances, came the Texas, Iowa, Oregon and Indiana, the little Gloucester lying in a corresponding position to the Vixen at the western horn of the crescent. In this distribution the Iowa was at a point about opposite the Santiago Harbor entrance and therefore the furthest from the shore. All the ships were headed in; lazily tossing in the long swell, with banked fires and motionless engines. The crews had been called to quarters and were grouped about, clad in their speckless white dress mustering suits and the captain and executive officer of each ship were below inspecting. Sunday service would soon be called and altogether it was a scene

of Sabbath peace at sea. It is well to fill the
mind with this idea of the rest and quiet of the
American ships on the one side and the alert
stillness of the Spanish fleet on the other, in order
to appreciate the extraordinary and startling
change that took place in a twinkling. It was a
transformation scene from the realms of Peace on
the Deep to the horror and turmoil of the Battlefield of the Demons of Discord, effected with a
suddenness, unique perhaps in the annals of warfare, and accompanied by such a swift and terrific
work of destruction as was certainly undreamed
of by the students of the possibilities of modern
war ships in action.

Complete as was the surprise caused by the
sudden appearance of Cervera's ships it speaks
volumes for the discipline of our men, under
what may be called relaxed conditions, that it
has been found almost impossible to decide
who really did first see the outcoming Spaniards. The lookouts on the Texas, Iowa and
Oregon all claim the distinction of being the
first to signal the discovery of Cervera's
attempt to escape, while, were this a boy's history
of the war, much pleasant importance might be
given to the claim of Joe Gaskin, a Newark lad
on board the Iowa, of whom it is said that he had
been watching all the morning for Cervera's ships

"because he had passed a good deal of the night thinking of them." The facts are that all three vessels signaled so simultaneously that the discoveries came as one; Joe Gaskin got his ten dollars as a special reward for vigilance, and it was the Oregon which put the discovery into effect. Without waiting to bend on and run up her signals the Oregon fired a six-pounder as an alarm and before its echoes had died away the string of parti-colored flags for signal 250, "The enemy is trying to escape," was flying from the masts of the Brooklyn, Texas, Iowa and Oregon. Smoke in the harbor had been seen many times and when it was noticed early this morning not much importance was attached to it. Toward 9 o'clock the wreaths of smoke which rose above the entrance hills grew more pronounced and still they were thought only to indicate activity among the tugs of the bay; but when at 9:35 a moving prow showed from behind Cay Smith and the next instant a black-hulled cruiser came into view the rousing, heart-prodding truth burst upon the fleet, and then it was that the signals went up and the curtain rose on the transformation scene.

Orders were issued of course, but they were not needed, for even while the ship-boys went flying through the gangways yelling that the Spaniards were coming out, the men had doffed their spick-and-span suits and stood stripped at their posts; drums were beating; battle-hatches and battle-ports were being put on; guns were loaded and trained and, downstairs, naked men were piling up the furnaces, hacking open the banked fires and coupling the boilers. As by a common impulse all this was done and as by a common impulse all the warships headed for the entrance.

It was the Maria Teresa, with Admiral Cervera on board, but not flying the admiral's pennant, which came first into view and it was the Maria Teresa that fired the first shot. As the cruiser cleared Socapa Point her forward turret belched black smoke and an eleven-inch shell came hurtling through the air and exploded as it touched the water between the Texas and Iowa. With its explosion came the American answer, an answer from all five warships and an answer that roared like the coming of a tornado and in whose midst, like that of a tornado, there was swift death and destruction.

For a time it was scarcely possible to decide on precise and separate lines of action or to quite make out the separate points of attack. The Spaniards came out shooting and with the discharges of their great guns, added to the volume

From photograph by J. C. Hemment.
The "Maria Teresa" after her surrender and as she lay a hulk of twisted

Copyright, 1898, by W. R. Hearst.

ns close into the Santiago shore. The precipitous and impassable nature of this shore and
rly brought out in this view.

of smoke from their funnels, the vessels were soon little more than moving smoke-clouds. They were rather as moving pillars of fire and smoke in each of which the faint outlines of a dark-colored, swift-moving warship could be seen, while between and across and around these smoke-clouds there rose and fell a moving line of fountains, where the great shells struck and threw up the sea. Then, to this bank of clouds and congregation of geysers, was added the on-coming wall of smoke with its spits of fire that marked the American fleet; and next the guns of the batteries added their smoke, until the whole sea and coast were covered with great rolling heaps and banks of cloud through which the position of the ships was marked by the flashes of the guns.

But moving clouds, lightning clouds as were the ships; and full of murk and lurid light as was the whole scene, out of it was soon evolved a fight of definiteness as to plan and of individuality as to contestants. Before that first terrific and wholesale broadside of the American fleet Cervera's plans melted away. With that frightful evidence coming from long range of what he would have to encounter at shorter range the Spanish fleet settled down to one object, that of making its escape. The Maria Teresa, the first to emerge, was also the first to set the new running. Scarcely had the cruiser cleared Socapa Point than over went her helm and away she sped, due west, heading for that section of the blockading squadron where the line was formed by the Vixen and Brooklyn. The Vixen, it will be remembered, lay close to shore and Cervera evidently thought, in this new and sudden plan, that he could slip by the Vixen without damage on account of her small size, and get away up the coast before the Brooklyn could close in and certainly before the great battleships could bring their massive forms into full action. As the long Castillian cruiser leaped forward the Vixen, with excellent discretion, scampered off to sea. The water was leaping high up the bows of the Brooklyn as she closed in, her long-range guns turned straight on the fleeing Spaniard. As the two vessels neared it looked for one desperate moment as though the Teresa intended to ram the Brooklyn, so wheeling with a rapidity that was of a part with the whole engagement the American flagship turned her bow westward and coupling on fresh boilers, ran parallel to the escaping cruiser, blazing away with all her starboard guns. But not alone from the Brooklyn did the Teresa receive her wounds, for even as the great battleships smothered inwards and westward they fired at so long a range that the resulting hits may be classed among the miracles of gunnery. The very first shot which the Brooklyn fired at the Teresa as the two came into parallel line cut the Spaniard's main water-supply pipe, but from the Texas and Oregon's giant guns she received the first of her death blows. One shell from the Oregon passed through her port quarter and exploded in the engine room, another landed on her stern and set her afire, while several thirteen-inch shells swept through her, each one at once a battering ram and a hail of far-reaching death. Then, as the Brooklyn brought the Teresa within range of her secondary battery the smaller shells of the American lodged and burst in her antagonist from stem to stern.

While the Teresa was thus receiving the brunt of the first fire, her lean, lank sisters had emerged from the entrance and were set with all their noses pointed west and racing for dear life, with the great American sea-hounds in hot pursuit. As each passed the fated Teresa she sent another shell or two into that doomed craft. There was no time to fight her, nor indeed was there any need to. The Teresa was out of the running. She had put her black muzzle out of Santiago Harbor at 9:35. At 10:10 she was a burning, riddled hulk, with her fire mains cut fore and aft and no way of putting out the blaze. Two of the thirteen-inch projectiles of the Texas had gone clear through her; an eight-inch shell from the Brooklyn had entered just forward of the beam on the port side and exploding had cleaned out the compartment with its four deck crews. One six-inch shell had carried away the bridge; another from the Brooklyn's forward turret struck the Spaniard amidships, exploded, tore down the bulkheads, destroyed stanchions, penetrated the deck, crippled two rapid-fire guns, killed fifteen or twenty men and carried panic everywhere.

For a moment the Teresa halted and veered, like a stricken man groping in the oncoming dark. To the sailors of our fleet, as they swept by it looked as though she were about to turn and were trying to stagger back into the shelter of the harbor, but when she had half swung a great gush of flame shot upward from her quarter, and it was seen that her commander was about to run her ashore. This he did at 10:35, having found a little cove, really a break in the coast-line, which the Cubans call Nima-Nama. As she struck the beach her colors went down, and the flames leaped up with renewed activity from the shock of her keel on the beach. And so ended the Infanta Maria Teresa, first-class cruiser, late of the Spanish navy.

Following the Teresa, and hugging the shore as that ship had done, came the Viscaya, and after her and parallel to her came on the Oregon and Texas, rapidly closing up the gap between them and the Brooklyn, while the Iowa turned in to look after the surrendered Teresa. The same tactics that had obtained in the battle with the Teresa were carried out in that with the Viscaya, except that the Brooklyn was now so far ahead that she was able to turn slightly in shore in such a way as to cut off the Viscaya's escape. But the cruiser never reached the line of the Brooklyn's offset. Schley, Clark and Philip thus kept up the race and the fire of the three ships was concentrated on this hapless hulk, while, as the Iowa turned in to look after the Teresa she let fly one spiteful shell at the Viscaya which struck the Spaniard's eleven-inch gun in the forward turret, cutting a furrow out of the side of the gun as though it had been done with a cold chisel. The shell exploded half way in the turret, making the vessel stagger and shake in every plate. Every gunner in the turret was killed and the place so choked with corpses that the new crew had to ship the dead through the ammunition hoist to the lower deck.

The Viscaya remained, however, the special prey of the Brooklyn and Oregon, the Texas having in her run paid most attention to the Oquendo.

Exclusive of the innumerable one-pounder and rapid-fire hits which swept the Viscaya's deck she was struck fourteen times by large projectiles and eleven times by six-pounders. The eight-inch guns of the Brooklyn and Oregon tore her structure above the armor belt into shreds, while the six-pounders of the two ships actually drove every Spaniard from the deck. Every rapid-fire gun on the Viscaya was silenced because every gunner had been either killed or crippled at his post; the military tops were filled with dead men; the surgeons had ceased to dress the wounded; the inside woodwork was ablaze and the hospital was a furnace. Men and officers acted like people bereft of their senses. The officers screamed their orders and the men rolled here and there like drunkards. Then, at 10:55, when the whole gun-deck was in flames and the magazines were in danger she, with her flag still flying, was headed for the shore at Acerradores, sixteen miles west of El Morro. Just as she turned for the shore, and when about four hundred yards from the beach, the Texas, in flying past in pursuit of the Colon, fired a shell from her after-turret. It hit the Viscaya a little forward of amidships just above the armor-belt, crashed through her side, crossed the gun-deck, ricocheting from compartment to compartment until it reached the

From photograph by J. C. Hemment.
Superstructure and main deck of the "Viscaya," showing the terrible

Copyright, 1898, by W. R. Hearst.
...tion caused by the exploding American shells and the succeeding fire.

forward torpedo-tubes one of which it exploded Torpedo and shell alike exploded indeed and while in its progress over the deck the shell killed eighty men, the double explosion blew out the starboard side of the cruiser and made her a complete wreck. And so ended the Viscaya.

The end of the Oquendo differed but little in its elements of horror from that of the two cruisers whose destruction has been described. Something appeared to be the matter with the machinery or engines of this vessel, for though the draught was being forced to such an extent that her funnel-tops were frequently crested with flames, she had fallen behind the Viscaya. In consequence of her comparative slowness everyone of our warships punished her as she swept along in the great parallel fight. In the case of the Oquendo, too, the pursuing ships had no need of long-range gunnery, but forged in closely to her and overwhelmed her with the fire of their secondary batteries. Only four eight-inch shells struck her and but two six-inch shells. On the other hand she was struck no less than forty-six times by our six-pounders, all of which entered above her armor-belt and exploded within, while the one-pounders from every vessel in the fleet seemed for a time to have been concentrated on her, these small but most mischievous missiles having plowed through, across and along her as a battery of machine-guns might have torn a regiment to pieces. She furnished an object lesson of the wonderful rapidity and accuracy of the fire of our small guns that was in its way as interesting and instructive as was the Teresa in showing what the Texas and Oregon could do in the way of landing a giant shell from a moving fortress into a flying target with a few miles between them.

Captain Eulate, who commanded the Oquendo, declared that it was the carnage caused by the secondary batteries of our ships, and mainly by the Brooklyn which led to his surrrender, the men being literally unable to work their guns. Eulate further reported that the long-range fighting, notwithstanding the heavier metal thrown, was as a child's love-pat compared with the thrashing received from the small guns. The rattle of the lighter shot on the steel decks, the incessant din, the constant flashing of exploding shells and the never ceasing shriek of the projectiles made up such a concatenation of horror that it seemed impossible to think of or hear anything outside of this devil's tattoo. The killing inside the ship was something too horrible for description. She caught on fire so many times and in so many places that the ironwork was scarcely bearable to the touch and the deck seemed red hot. Every beam was twisted and torn from its original position. It was absolutely beyond human endurance to hold out further; she was a shambles above and below; the track of the shells was marked by human remains. One eight-inch shell struck the forward turret at the gun opening; every man in the turret was killed and the officer in the firing-hood was blown to pieces. The engineer force was penned up because of the battle-gratings being jammed. So having reached a point opposite the beach where the Teresa was run, she was headed in about five hundred yards above her helpless consort, with flames rising fiercely from stem to stern. And so, with explosions that still further wrecked her shattered sides and deck, the Almirante Oquendo was finished.

There remained then the torpedo-destroyers and the Cristobal Colon. The plans of Admiral Cervera were being wofully interfered with. For a time, and really in due sequence as the death of the Colon came later, the desperate running of that swift cruiser can be passed over while attention is paid to the fate of the destroyers—those untried craft concerning whose possibilities so much had been written and feared. The last of the cruisers was two miles from the entrance when the Pluton came into view, closely followed by the Furor. Their low black forms seemed to waver for a moment and their bows were pointed eastward; then, following the course of the cruisers they, too, headed for the west. Blood-curdling tales had been told of what these wicked little craft would do; of their thirty-knot speed; of their magical ability to maneuver and of their power to launch a torpedo and get away unscathed with the swiftness of an enraged wasp. Instead of all this, the reality was two wavering little boats which could not even run away, but which slowly moved into the shadow of the shore as though seeking to avoid observation. On our side there was no apparent thought as to the ferocious possibilities of the destroyers, for the Oregon scarcely deigned to pepper them as she dashed to the front; the Texas treated them to a secondary battery shower as she too moved west; the Iowa, running neck and neck with the Oregon, swerved a little to tear the stern of the Furor to pieces with one fierce shell and then passed on, contemptuously leaving the completer destruction of the craft to the little Gloucester.

The Gloucester had been the millionaire Morgan's yacht, known as Corsair No. 2, and even as a converted gunboat was as harmless a looking pirate as ever put the quietus to a couple of distressed Spanish sea-bravos. The captain of the

Gloucester was Lieutenant Harry P. Wainwright, who had been the last man to leave the hulk of the Maine as she settled into the silt of Havana Harbor. Dashing right inside of the line of our cruisers until she was close under the guns of El Morro, and in the full fire of those batteries, of the stern-chasers of the fleeing cruisers and of the possibilities of the terrible things the destroyers could do, the little yacht darted in to tackle them at close quarters. Carrying four six-pounder rapid-fire guns, four three-pounder rapid-fire guns and two small Colt automatics and with a complement of ninety-three officers and men the little unarmored 800-ton yacht started in to finish up the two Spanish fighting craft, each as long as she, each built to destroy, each carrying two fourteen-pound, two six-pound and four one-pound rapid-fire guns, and two fourteen-inch torpedo tubes, with a total complement of one hundred and thirty-four men. The gun work on the Gloucester was record-making; empty shells rolled about the deck, breech-locks grew so hot that they refused to work, the men were stripped naked and though the Spaniards shot valiantly in their attempt to sink their tiny antagonist, not a shot struck her. Pushing forward until within five hundred yards of the destroyers, firing now at one now at the other the Gloucester pressed on. Suddenly there was a flash, not that of a gun, on board the Pluton and she began to settle. At the sight of this catastrophe the Furor circled back to El Morro as though running away from her wounded sister, and then circled back as though ashamed of her conduct and as though she were returning to assist in the Pluton's dying struggles. But again she turned, and it was then seen that she was drifting and simply moving in a circle because of a jammed helm. For all this the Gloucester kept up her withering fire until the Furor went down by the head and sank in deep water just west of Cabanas, while the Pluton managed to get close enough to run ashore. Wainwright had remembered the Maine.

Among those saved was Lieutenant Boado-Suances of the Pluton and some days after, when he was able to think clearly, for the horror of his experience almost made him mad, he told his story. Of shattered steam-pipes and escaping steam scalding to death the engineers and stokers as they stood; of men cut in twain by fragments of giant shells; of the boats thrown on their beam ends from the force of the shells' impact and torn to pieces from the explosions; of other shells whose path could be marked by splashes in the sea as they came bounding toward them, sure as death and straight as an arrow, at whose sight men screamed shrilly in their fear.

There remained then the Colon. For a time it looked as though the plan for her escape by running inside the line of the other cruisers might be carried to a successful conclusion. In the din and smother and roar of the other engagements this fleet ship coursed westward, gaunt-looking and rapid as a hound. But there were sharp eyes and nimble minds on board the American ships. The Spaniard had reeled off many a good knot in her flight and of her pursuers all but two were left moderately well behind—the Brooklyn and the Oregon, a cruiser and a battleship. In their running fight the two Americans pressed on after the Spaniard in a line that would have brought them broadside along her—the Spaniard following the trend of the coast. But this coast dipped into bay which ended in Cape Cruz to the westward. Schley saw the cape and immediately turned out and headed for it, and when the Spaniard saw this move he knew that his case was hopeless. As the Brooklyn swung out the Oregon put on a burst of speed and followed the Colon, and it was at this time that the battleship made for herself a record among the fighting machines of the world, and set the fleet a-roaring.

Put together like a watch they knew her to be; steady as an East Indiaman she had proved herself to be in her ever-memorable voyage up and down the oceans of the New World; big as a city block of buildings they could see her to be, but when this monstrous floating fortress went leaping over and through the waves like a clippership and that without any apparent effort, her smoke-stacks being crested only with the faintest haze, men threw up their hands in amazement.

From fighting mast to fighting mast the Oregon and the Brooklyn signaled the range to and fro and both began firing. It was then one o'clock P.M. and the distance between battleship and cruiser was six thousand yards. As the Oregon dashed along in the general pursuit of and fight with the other Spaniards she looked indeed a floating fortress, firing fore, aft and abeam at once, but now she settled down into a steady target-practice. Now, too, the Colon having seen the error of her way was making every effort to slip past Cape Cruz, beyond which lay safety. Every pound of steam was crowded on and she was going a nineteen-knot gait. But tear through the water as she might, the long slim Brooklyn was swiftly and surely getting between her and the headland. Captain Clark's great shells were beginning to fall around her, while behind the Oregon the

Texas could be seen pounding along in her wake under a forced draught. The Oregon's thirteen-inch shells fell nearer and nearer to the Colon and the Spaniard was headed for the shore and her flag hauled down.

Hers was the most inglorious end of all the Spanish fleet. She was in good fighting commission when run ashore. Having kept behind the other ships for protection, the Colon was hit with large projectiles about six times, these having been made by the Brooklyn and Oregon. One eight-inch shell went clean through her without exploding, one five-inch hit her just above the armor-belt and one six-inch struck her on the bow, but no blow was fatal or even serious.

When the Colon turned in and ran her nose on the coral keys about the mouth of the Rio Tarquino, forty-eight miles west of Santiago, she was a surrendered ship in good condition. When the Americans reached her she was a wreck and had been wantonly made so. The breech-locks of the guns had been torn out and thrown overboard. Every inlet for water had been opened and the wrecking-gang of the Merrimac had not worked more religiously and efficiently to sink that collier than did the officers and men of the Colon to wreck and scuttle her after surrender. Only one life had been lost and she had less than twenty men wounded.

The New York's share in the fight was that of an observer. It will be remembered that she had gone down to Siboney for a Sunday morning call on Shafter. At half-past nine the sound of heavy guns reached the flagship and turning westward the bridge-officer saw and reported "Firing from the eastern and western batteries and the ships returning it." A moment's confusion, a skurrying of orderlies and the New York's bow was brought around for Santiago. Eight knots was all she could make at first, only two boilers being in use, but new fires were started, the forward engines coupled and as the deck was cleared for action she soon gathered speed. As she swept by the Resolute that gunboat was sent back to Siboney to cable to Playa del Este to order up the Massachusetts and all other vessels thereabouts, and the torpedo boat Ericsson was gathered up in the westward run. As she came opposite El Morro the flagship fired her forward four-inch guns, four shots in all and these were her only shots for the day. They were aimed at the Terror and one was thought to have struck the upper works of that destroyer. The others went wide. As the flagship swept on, the destroyers were seen to be total wrecks, and Wainwright was busy succoring his enemies.

Five miles beyond the harbor entrance,

Sampson saw the Spanish flagship Infanta Maria Teresa beached and flying a white flag; less than a mile beyond at Juan Gonzales, Sampson saw the Almirante Oquendo beached and ablaze; opposite Acerradores, Sampson passed the Viscaya ashore and blazing like the Oquendo. What Sampson had so far seen of the Spanish fleet was a succession of battered and blazing hulks. There remained only the Colon, and the flagship pressed on to be at least in at the death of that cruiser, but when the flagship reached the Rio Tarquino the Colon had surrendered. Sampson there received Schley's report of his glorious victory, took charge of the transfer of prisoners and placed Lieutenant-Commander James G. Cogswell, executive officer of the Oregon, in command of the Colon.

It was thought that the Colon might be saved and the Vixen was set to tow her inshore, but the tug could not move the Spaniard's huge bulk. Next the flagship muzzled her sharp prow with a rope fender and, it being then night time, set the glare of her searchlight on the Spaniard's starboard quarter and moved her own engines ahead. Slowly the Colon swung around under this great pressure and it was hoped that a new vessel would be added there and then to our navy. Suddenly, however, the Colon rolled over on her port side with her starboard guns pointing straight and silently upward. So ended the Colon, and in this way was the New York in at the death.

Having thus made an end of Cervera's fleet and done their best to blow the Spanish crews into eternity, the American commanders remembered that it was Sunday and that the enemy being in a pit it was their duty as members of the church militant to drag him out thereof. All up and down the coast, therefore, where had raged the tumult of battle the boats and launches of our warships were busy in the work of succor. The Gloucester's boats rescued the survivors of the burning Pluton as they swam and then steamed to the beach on which were gathered the survivors of the Teresa. Among these was Admiral Cervera, a short, paunchy gray-bearded gentleman, who in his underclothes stepped forward and surrendered. He explained his personality and was transferred to the Iowa where he received the honors of his rank and a new suit of clothes. The Indiana lowered her boats and at different points along the shore picked up seven officers and two hundred and three men. From the sinking Viscaya and the beach near her and the sea about her, the Iowa picked up thirty-eight officers and two hundred and thirty-eight men; while W. R. Hearst, who with that originality of enterprise which had made him and his paper, the New York Journal, of national prominence, and who had gone to Cuba as the war correspondent of his own paper, rounded up a squad of the Viscaya's men and delivered them out of the hands of the Cubans into those of the officers of the St. Louis. So it went on for hours, for the rest of the day and the coming night in truth, with shelter and courtesy to the officers, with care and comfort to the men, with nursing and medical attendance for the wounded, and with decent burial for the dead.

It was the same spirit of mercy to the vanquished which led Captain John W. Philip of the Texas to forbid his men to cheer when the Viscaya ran up the white flag. So long as there was any fight in the Spaniard he was to be battered and pelted and torn, but when the token of submission was flying over a vessel that had been changed from a swift-moving thing full of life and action into something that was at once a furnace and a charnel-house, it was a triumph to be sure, but not a time for noisy jubilation. So, "Don't cheer men," cried Captain Philip, as the jackies began to yell and caper, "those poor devils are dying."

It was in a tenderer and still higher spirit that this same Captain Philip, when the fight was over,

did something that showed him possessed of a
moral courage as great in degree as the physical
courage that had kept him on the bridge all
through the engagement in the fierce give-and-
take fight between the mighty engines of destruction. The men with their stripped bodies
black with the grime of battle; the decks strewn
with the splintered evidences of fight; the great
guns still steaming, with their breech-locks turned
open to the air; the turret crews stumbling out
of their steel furnaces; and the delirium of victory
over all—surely this was a time and these were
the elements for the noise and rejoicing of material things, the time to yell for themselves and
their good ship. But to Captain Philip it was
something more than a victory of men and material and beckoning to the crew to gather around
him he stood straight before them, with a clear
unflinching light in his little beady eyes and taking off his cap said:

"I want to make public acknowledgment here
that I believe in God, the Father Almighty, and
I want all you officers and men to lift your hats
and from your hearts offer silent thanks to the
Almighty."

Plain, simple words and uttered with the plain
simple faith of a child; yet the heart of the people has been moved more deeply by this avowal

of the Lord God of Gideon than by all the other thrilling incidents of the great fight of July 3d—whatever may be the cause of the moving, whether the sentimentality that follows the reading of great deeds as a transient feeling, or the inherent Puritanism of the nation as a settled fact.

The statistics of this great sea-battle almost bore out the Philipian idea of a providential guardianship. The Spanish losses were five hundred killed, sixteen hundred prisoners, mostly wounded, and the total destruction of four cruisers and two torpedo-boat destroyers, representing a value of over twenty million dollars. The American list of casualties stood at one man killed, chief yeoman Geo. H. Ellis of the Brooklyn, and two wounded, and superficial damages which it would cost a few thousand dollar to repair. But the hard logic of fact shows that the destruction of the Spanish fleet and the escape of ours was due to relative gunnery; to good gunnery on our side and to bad gunnery on theirs. From the moment of the fleet's emerging from Santiago to the beaching of the Colon, the Spaniards fired as best they might. But most of the Spanish shots fell over our ships and it was the expert belief of our officers that the enemy did not change their range.

Another reason why the Spanish gunnery was harmless lay in the demoralization of the gunners. As we have seen, the Spanish officers acknowledged that the scenes on board their ships were those of cumulative horrors growing out of the din and slaughter of battle, but the men have stated that each ship was a drunken inferno; that gunners and stokers were plied with rum; that treasure was scattered about the decks; that the cannoneers reeled drunkenly about their guns and that the officers shot them down as they reeled. For the credit of humanity it is hoped the stories are exaggerated; to the shame of Spain it must be said the evidence is strongly against her.

Cervera himself, as he stood on the quarter-deck of the Iowa, furnished the key to the situation, when he said "the rapidity and accuracy of the American fire was almost incredible." That was just it. It was the men behind the guns who won this famous victory and the Spaniard was smashed by American gunnery.

Here are a few concrete facts to remember in this connection, given even at the risk of repetition: Cervera came out at 9:35 A. M. At 10:10 the Teresa was on fire. At 10:15 the Furor and Pluton were blown up or sinking. At 10:30 the Oquendo was beached and had sur-

The Fall of Santiago.

rendered. At 10:35 the Teresa had followed suit. At 11 the Viscaya hauled down her colors. At 1:15 the Colon had given up the fight and had been wrecked. Including the chase of the Colon it had taken us three hours and forty minutes to destroy the Spanish squadron. Leaving out the chase of the Colon, the fight was won in one hour and ten minutes, while such was the condition of the enemy that victory was assured us in thirty minutes. During that decisive thirty minutes we fired over seventeen hundred shots, the reports of the discharges being literally incessant. By large-sized missiles the Oquendo was struck fifty-five times; the Teresa thirty-seven times; the Viscaya twenty-five and the Colon six; while the hits by the smaller guns were in each case countless. The fight started at a range of six thousand yards, while at two thousand and two thousand five hundred yards two torpedo boats and two cruisers were annihilated. The closest fighting of the whole engagement, though this record may bring sorrow to the artists who persist in laying their battling ships alongside each other, was at eleven hundred yards, when the Brooklyn and Viscaya were settling accounts.

As to the other lessons of the great fight; of the mute evidences furnished by the Oquendo of how a ship looks when riven by an internal explosion as compared to that furnished by the Maine; of the incalculable damage possible when modern war ships meet; of the unspeakable horrors that were found within the charred hulks of the Spanish ships and of the great leap forward which the United States navy made in the appreciation of Europe's War Lords—of all these things much could be and doubtless will be said, but there is no place for it here.

CHAPTER X.

HOW TORAL SURRENDERED MORE THAN WAS ASKED FOR.

When Shafter sent his ultimatum of shell or surrender to Toral at 8:20 on the morning of July 3, Toral replied with a refusal to acknowledge himself beaten, and it was for the exchange of these communications between the two commanders that the white flag was set up between the opposing lines to the surprise of our men on San Juan hill, as has been described in a previous chapter. The reply of Toral to Shafter's demand was as follows:

Santiago de Cuba, July 3.
"To His Excellency the General Commanding the forces of the United States, San Juan River:
"Sir: I have the honor to reply to your communication of to-day, written at 8:20 a.m. and received at 1 p.m., demanding the surrender of this city; in the contrary case in announcing to me that you will bombard the city, and that I advise the foreigners and women and children

that they must leave the city before 10 o'clock to-morrow morning.

"It is my duty to say to you that this city will not surrender, and that I will inform the foreign consuls and inhabitants of the contents of your message.

"Very respectfully,
"JOSE TORAL,
"Commander-in-Chief, Fourth Corps."

When Toral sent this brave reply Cervera was a fighting or fleeing possibility and something, that something to which the Spaniard is always clinging, might be done to relieve the beleaguered city. Pando was coming too, Pando with his fresh army from Holquin; the gunnery of our ships had not so far wrought much havoc to the city or forts—and so he sent his answer. He informed the British, Portuguese, Chinese and Norwegian consuls of the threatened bombardment, and in consonance with this notification these officials came to the American lines and preferred the request that the bombardment be postponed until 10 o'clock A.M. Thursday the 5th, asking further that the non-combatants, numbering between fifteen thousand and twenty thousand, might be allowed to occupy the town of El Caney. To this request Shafter acceded, and sent the following notification to Toral:

"Commanding General Spanish forces, Santiago de Cuba, July 3.

"Sir: In consideration of the request of the consuls and officers of your city for delay in carrying out my intention to fire on the city, and in the interest of the poor women and children, who will suffer very greatly by their enforced departure from the city, I have the honor to announce that I will delay such action solely in their interest until noon of the 5th, providing during the interval your forces make no demonstration whatever upon mine. I am, with great respect, your obedient servant,

"W. R. SHAFTER."

When the news of the destruction of Cervera's fleet reached our headquarters Shafter not only sent it to the front, where it was received with a round of cheers that stretched from one end of the line to the other and with the blare of the only band that had managed to keep together, but with excellent policy sent it also to the commander of the Spanish forces in Santiago.

Whether the lookout at El Morro had reported to Santiago the woful result of Cervera's attempt to escape; whether he had not been able to make out clearly the full extent of the horror in all its smother of smoke and its confusion of rushing ships; or whether Shafter's brief bulletin was the first intimation received by Linares and Toral-that Spain had lost another fleet—all these are points that have not as yet been definitely settled. It is definitely known, however, that the reception of the news of this additional disaster caused the most poignant grief to the Spanish commanders, and had it not been for their pachydermatous pride and their strict adherence to the punctilios of deference to higher authorities, the demand of Shafter would have been there and then acceded to.

As it was, Governor-General Blanco was communicated with at Havana, and in obedience to the suggestion received from him Toral proposed that the truce still continue and that, during it, commissioners be appointed from both sides to discuss the question of capitulation.

In deference to this small step pacifically forward the day of general attack by land and sea was postponed, for while Shafter professed to the Spaniards that he was opposed to the roundabout road to surrender along which commissioners would possibly travel, he saw at once that this parleying on the part of Toral pointed but one way.

The situation within each line was at this time thoroughly characteristic. On the American side, the persistent strengthening of the position

Maj. Gen. W. B. Shafter.

as the practical advantage of the extension of time; on the Spanish side, increased distress and a desperate evasion of the inevitable. Toral's next move in this impractical direction was the request to Shafter that the cable operators, who had left Santiago on the first notification of bombardment, might be permitted to return to the city in order that the situation might be laid before the government at Madrid. Shafter consented to this, but, as a rider, notified Toral that too much time was being consumed in preliminaries, and that a Yes or No to the demand for surrender must be received before noon of July 9, or the threatened bombardment would surely begin.

The cable operators returned to Santiago on July 8, and when the 9th came Toral was ready with another move for delay and asked that instead of a bombardment the American commander consider this proposition: that he, Toral, evacuate the city, provided his forces be permitted to retire immediately to Holquin. Shafter refused to consider this suggestion, and ordered Randolph's Brigade which had just landed to march to the front and to bring its field artillery with it.

Then Toral sent back to say that he had been ordered to make this offer by his government over the cable which Shafter had so generously placed at his disposal, and that he had been further requested to ask that the suggestion be laid before the government at Washington. Then Shafter saw that he had been deftly cornered, again postponed the bombardment, forwarded the request to Washington and strengthened his lines around the Holquin road. In this fashion it happened that by the curiously circuitous way of the single cable from Santiago that had escaped capture—for oddly enough it was only found, and that accidentally, by the anchor of the Massachusetts off Aguadores on the day of the surrender—and so it happened, I say, that over this cable via the generals in command on the battlefield and our appropriated cable from Playa del Este, the authorities at Washington and Madrid were in communication for the first time since Woodford had received his passports. In the same roundabout way, but in the most direct language, Shafter was instructed to inform Toral, for the benefit of Sagasta, that the unconditional surrender of Santiago must be granted, or fire would be opened along the entire American line on the morning of July 11.

Possibly Toral thought that in view of the many postponements he had secured this, new ultimatum would not be rigorously insisted on. In this, however, he was mistaken, for when July 11 came, with it came the thunder of the great guns from the ships, the cough of the Vesuvius and the earthquake result of its dynamite shells, and the roar of Randolph's heavy siege pieces. Some of the giant shells from Sampson's ships reached the city, and the men at San Juan could see whole squares crumble where the steel projectiles exploded. The firing from the lines was mainly directed against the Spanish trenches and was but feebly replied to. Of loss of life there was little, Santiago being practically deserted by everyone except the garrison, and El Caney and the inland roads therefrom to Siboney being crowded with tens of thousands of refugees. It was intended as an object lesson, as an emphatic reminder that an answer to a certain question was being delayed. Yet with all the havoc caused by the bombardment and with a full knowledge of their condition, the Spanish leaders obstinately clung to their determination to surrender in obedience to commands from Madrid and not on the demand of Washington. Then it was that Linares, whose pride was broked down by sickness and pain, sent the following appeal to his government, one of the most pathetic revelations of the Spanish helplessness and hopelessness at Santiago that can be imagined:

"Official cablegram, July 12, 1898.

"To the Minister of War from the General-in-Chief of the Division of Santiago de Cuba:

"Although confined to my bed by great weakness and in much pain, the situation of the long-suffering troops here occupies my mind to such an extent that I deem it my duty to address Your Excellency that the state of affairs may be explained.

"Enemy's lines very near the town and on account of the nature of the ground our lines are in full view from them. Troops weak; sick in considerable proportion not sent to hospitals owing to the necessity for keeping them in the intrenchments. Horses and mules without the usual allowance of forage. In the midst of the wet season, with twenty hours' daily fall of rain in the trenches, which are simply ditches dug in the ground, without any permanent shelter for the men, who have nothing but rice to eat and no means of changing or drying their clothing. Considerable losses; field officers and company officers killed, wounded and sick, deprive the troops of necessary orders in critical moments.

"Under these circumstances it is impossible to fight our way out, because in attempting to do so our force would be lacking one-third of the men, who could not leave, and we would be weakened beside by casualties caused by the enemy, resulting finally in a veritable disaster, without saving our diminished battalions. In order to get out, protected by the Holquin division, it will be necessary for me to break the enemy's line. For this operation the Holquin division will require eight days and will have to bring a large amount of rations, which it is impossible to transport. The solution of the question is ominously imposed upon us.

"Surrender is inevitable and we can only succeed in prolonging the agony. The sacrifice is useless, and the enemy understand this. They see our lines, and theirs being well established and close up, they tire out our men without exposing themselves, as they did yesterday, when they cannonaded us on land with such an elevation that we were unable to see their batteries, and from the sea by a squadron which had a perfect range and bombarded the town in sections with mathematical precision.

"The complete exodus of the inhabitants, insular as well as peninsular, includes the occupants of the public offices, with few exceptions. There only remains the clergy, and they to-day started to leave the town with the archbishop at their head.

"The defenders here cannot now begin a campaign full of enthusiasm and energy. They came here three years ago struggling against the climate, privations and fatigue, and now they are placed in these sad circumstances, where they have no food, no physical force and no means of recuperating. The ideal for them is lacking, because they are defending the property of those that have abandoned it and of those that now are being fed by the American forces. The honor of the army has its limits, and I appeal to the opinion of the whole nation as to whether these long-suffering troops have not kept it safely many times since May 18, when they were subjected to the first cannonade. If it is necessary that the sacrifice be endured, for reasons of which I am ignorant, or that some one shall assume the responsibility of the unfortunate termination which I have anticipated and mentioned in a number of telegrams, I faithfully offer myself on the altars of my country for the one, and for the other I will retain the command for the purpose of signing the surrender, for my modest reputation is of little value as compared with the country's interests. LINARES."

But pitiful as was the condition of the Spanish soldiers, that of the American forces was also bad, was indeed wretched. When the great fight was over, from the firing line along San Juan's crest all down the muddy, sodden road to Siboney was an unending though halting string of maimed and shattered men; the ambulance-carts—crowded like a potter's field—jolted down to the hospitals; the surgeon's field-tents were overrun and the center of patient men in pain; up and down the eight wearyful miles of mire, white-faced lads were dragging themselves with aimless looks on their faces; and anywhere, wherever they might be found, writhing Spaniards were being tenderly but hurriedly cared for by our surgeons, while a surprised look crept over the poor fellows' faces, or quiet Spaniards were being hurriedly

Gen. Linares.

buried when no look could come over their faces at all. Our trenches too, like those of the Spaniards, were ditches of muddy water and our men had to stand in these, wet from the waist downward and parboiled from the waist upward. Despite the truce, incessant alertness was necessary and trenches were constantly being deepened and extended. The commissariat was deficient, and the need of the necessities from which the men had debarrassed themselves on their march to the front was again acutely felt. Sickness was beginning to appear—had appeared in fact—an ugly persistent malarious fever which seized the men like a foe in the dark, wrestled with them and left them helpless. Then from crowded El Caney and the embowered pest-hole of Siboney rumors came that the dreaded yellow-jack had appeared, and all too soon these rumors were found to be well-founded. First a man here and there crawled to the doctor with all the telltale symptoms upon him. Then they were found by batches, pest-camps were established, and all too late Siboney was burned out of existence. The excitement of fight was gone and in its place was present the horrible depression that came alike as a collapse after such a tremendous physical and nervous strain and as the natural accompaniment of the knowledge that the plague had appeared and that the Spaniards' invisible ally was at work.

Things were bad enough, wretched enough with us indeed. But here the similarity of conditions ended. Back of us was a strong, rich government, with one fixed object in view; a victorious navy with no floating foe to take account of; reinforcements on a score of hurrying transports and others already at the Cuban base of supplies, and best of all the great American heart which beat in unison with that of the army. On the other hand was an army without support of navy, with its local reinforcements cut off, and hampered by a divided government, incapable alike of rendering assistance or appreciating the desperate bravery of its despairing soldiers.

General Miles arrived almost on the echo of the bombardment, and when another flag of truce appeared in the valley that lay between San Juan and Santiago, and a message was sent to the American headquarters repeating the proposition for the appointment of commissioners, the return proposition was made that in such a discussion the chiefs themselves should meet. A conference of these was set for July 14, at noon, and at that hour Generals Miles, Shafter and Wheeler met General Toral and aids underneath

a cieba tree halfway between the lines. Toral informed our generals that he had received instructions from Captain-General Blanco to consent that the commissioners should have plenary power to negotiate the terms of a surrender.

For himself, Toral named as commissioners General Escario, Lieutenant-Colonel Fortan and Albert Mason, the British Vice-Consul; while Shafter named Generals Wheeler and Ewers and Captain Miley. The commissioners met under the same cieba tree at 2 o'clock in the afternoon, Toral being also present. Though so near a settlement, the dilatory and evasive tactics of the Spaniards were consistently manifest. It was stated by Toral that the sanction of Blanco to the proceedings was but preliminary, and that the consent of Madrid would be necessary to complete the bargain. This the American commissioners declared to be unsatisfactory and wrong, and in their direct fashion presented thirteen articles of surrender to Toral for his acceptance or rejection. But no such direct methods were in Toral's mind; and in the flood of talk that followed, the American commissioners were so swamped from the plain ground of solid fact that they actually agreed to proceed to the consideration of the preliminaries, leaving open the question of whether or not the Spanish forces had surrendered. On this undefined basis the discussion of the thirteen articles was proceeded with, much to the enjoyment of the voluble Spaniards and the growing impatience of the Americans.

At length when midnight was passed and a crystallization of result seemed as far off as ever, General Wheeler insisted on a test of *bona fides*, and the articles were taken up seriatim and each was dealt with until it was accepted. When all had been thus declared satisfactory, Wheeler further insisted that the Spanish commissioners should affix their signatures to the articles and this, much against their will they did, in the early morning hours of July 15. But satisfactory as this was, back of it all remained the unpleasant fact that nothing was concluded. Toral had insisted that everything was preliminary and subject to orders from Madrid, and Toral carried the day. There was no apprehension, however, on the American side as to the outcome, and the concession to Toral's dignity was not regarded as calculated to jeopardize the result. Next day the atmosphere was cleared up by the receipt of a dispatch from Toral saying that his government had "authorized him to capitulate." This one phrase was intelligible both in its original Spanish and in the unique translation which lies in

The Fall of Santiago. 241

the archives of the War Department, but the rest of it was a mystery. The document reads as follows:

"SANTIAGO DE CUBA, July 16.
"To His Excellency, Commander-in-Chief of the American Forces.
"Excellent Sir: I am now authorized by my government to capitulate.
"I have the honor to so apprise you, and requesting you that you designate hour and place where my representatives shall appear to compare with those of Your Excellency to effect the articles of capitulation on the basis of what has been agreed upon to this date in due time.
"I wish to manifest my desire to know the resolutions of the United States Government respecting the return of army, so as to note on the capitulation, also the great courtesy of Your Great Graces and return for their great generosity and impulse for the Spanish soldiers, and allow them to return to the Peninsula with the honors the American army do them, the honor to acknowledge as dutifully descended.
"JOSE TORAL,
"General Commanding Fourth Army Corps.
"(Signed) "GENERAL SHAFTER,
"Commanding American Forces."

Whether it was during the many conferences in which interpreters of varying degrees of inaccuracy were employed as the medium of informing one side what the other side said; whether neither side quite understood the literal import of the various dispatches of demand and evasion; which of these conditions lies as the cause of the result, this amazing fact remains that when Toral surrendered, our leaders found that he had not only consented to a capitulation of the city of Santiago and its army, but that he intended to give up what was practically the whole of Eastern Cuba and its armies. Miles has stated that he was surprised. And so was indeed every member of the commission, but each man kept silence with the imperturbability of a practiced poker-player whose bluff had not been called. The terms of Toral's capitulation, in brief were these:

"Surrender of all Spanish forces in that part of Santiago Province which lies east of a straight line drawn from Aceradores, on the south coast, to Dos Palmas, in the interior, and thence to Sagua de Tanamo, on the north coast; estimated at nearly twenty-five thousand men, of which number twelve thousand had not been engaged.

"Surrender of all war material then in the described district. All artillery and batteries at the harbor entrance and gunboat in harbor to be left intact.

"Officers to retain their side arms and personal property.

Street Scene in Santiago taken after the American occupation.

The Fall of Santiago.

"Privates to give up their arms of all kinds and retain their personal property only.

"Toral authorized to take away the military archives belonging to the described district.

"The United States to transport all the surrendered troops back to Spain as soon as possible, embarking them near the garrisons they then occupied.

"The volunteer and guerrilla forces allowed to remain in Cuba, if they wish, under parole, during the present war.

"Toral's army to march out of Santiago with honors of war, depositing their arms at a point mutually agreed upon, to await disposition of United States Government, our commissioners recommending that they be returned to the soldiers.

"The existing municipal authorities to continue in control of the garrison cities until the Spanish troops were embarked.

"Mines and torpedoes at mouth of Santiago Harbor to be removed by Spanish.

"No Cubans to be allowed to enter Santiago until after evacuation.

"Refugees from Santiago to be allowed to return to their homes.

"Miss Clara Barton and Red Cross agents to be allowed to enter the city."

The time of surrender was fixed at 9 o'clock of the morning of July 17. At that hour Generals Shafter, Lawton, Wheeler, Kent and Hines, accompanied by their staffs and escorted by cavalry and infantry detachments went at an easy pace down the winding road from San Juan hill to the famous cieba tree, and sent an aid to the Spanish lines to notify General Toral that Shafter was ready to receive the surrender of Santiago. Toral, white-haired and sad-faced, almost instantly appeared with his staff and about a hundred picked men and came loping up the road. As the two commanders neared, the trumpeters on both sides saluted with flourishes, while from a Spanish battery a salute was fired and from our troops lined up along the trenches there went a stalwart American cheer. Toral unbuckled his sword and saluting, handed it to Shafter saying:

"Hago entrega al General Shafter, del ejercito Americano, la ciudad y fortalejas de la ciudad de Santiago."
("I make over to General Shafter, Commander of the American Army, the citadel and fortifications of the City of Santiago.")

To this Shafter replied: "I receive the city in the name of the Government of the United States."

With this acceptance, however, Toral's sword was handed back to him and then with a clatter of hoofs and a rattle of American scabbards

First United States coaling station in the Harbor of Santiago after its occupation by the American troops.

Shafter and Toral rode side by side into the city at the head of their dual escort. At its entrance the civil authorities and church dignitaries in their glistening vestments came forward to meet conquered and conquerors. Along the ill-paved streets, and past the yellow-walled houses, the procession passed until the Plaza de la Reina was reached. On one side rose the Mauresque Palace, on the other the great cathedral, and on the other two the broad-verandaed clubhouse of San Carlos and the Café de la Venus. Stretching from side to side of the Plaza was a long blue line of the Ninth Infantry and a picked troop of the Second Cavalry. Well to the front was the Sixth Cavalry Band; massed on the flagging before the palace were Shafter and his retinue.

As the cathedral clock struck twelve every eye was turned to the red-tiled roof of the palace, from the flagpole of which streamed out the yellow and crimson flag of Spain, but before the last stroke of noon that standard came fluttering down, never to be again raised, and in its place ran up the brilliant folds of the Stars and Stripes. As the full standard broke out in the breeze the troops came to order arms; the cavalry band broke into the "Star Spangled Banner;" there was a faint cheer from the wondering people who pressed against the Plaza rails and crowded to the barred windows of the houses; while from the American lines drifted in the distant boom of Capron's saluting batteries and the muffled roar of our cheering troops.

Santiago had fallen.

THE END.

www.ingramcontent.com/pod-product-compliance
Lightning Source LLC
Chambersburg PA
CBHW022023240426
43667CB00042B/1075